Seventy Images of Grace in the Epistles . . .

Seventy Images of Grace in the Epistles . . .

—— That Make All the Difference in Daily Life ——

Norma Cook Everist

Foreword by Martin E. Marty

CASCADE *Books* • Eugene, Oregon

SEVENTY IMAGES OF GRACE IN THE EPISTLES . . .
That Make All the Difference in Daily Life

Cascade Books
An Imprint of Wipf and Stock Publishers
199 W. 8th Ave., Suite 3
Eugene, OR 97401

New Revised Standard Version of the Bible, copyright 1989, Division of Christian Education of the National Council of Churches of Christ in the United States of America. Used by permission. All rights reserved.
www.wipfandstock.com

ISBN 13: 978-1-62564-739-9

Cataloging-in-Publication data:

Everist, Norma Cook, 1938–

  Seventy images of grace in the Epistles . . . : that make all the difference in daily life / Norma Cook Everist.

  xxviii + 184 p. ; 23 cm. —Includes bibliographical references and indexes.

  ISBN 13: 978-1-62564-739-9

  1. Bible. Epistles—Theology. 2. Grace (Theology). I. Marty, Martin E., 1928–. II. Title.

BS2777 .E94 2015

Manufactured in the U.S.A.   07/02/2015

To Burton
who lives by grace

Contents

Chapter 6
Beyond Suffering toward Hope | 100

Chapter 7
People Transformed to Be Change Agents in the World | 122

Chapter 8
More Images than We Can Imagine | 145

Foreword

"To Iowa"

Two words, *those* two words, appear in isolation on the first page, the dedication page, of the memorable novel *Lila* by the celebrated author Marilynne Robinson. Most authors use their dedication pages to thank or give credit to family members, teachers, or other inspiring people. Thanking or giving credit to a *thing* is a different matter. Why does a state deserve Dedication Page privileges? And, of all states, why Iowa?

Those who know the work of Robinson and the fact that she teaches at the famed Iowa Writers' Workshop well recognize that Iowa helps shape the outlook and work of this novelist. To many Americans from the coasts, Iowa is "flyover country." To some traveled sophisticates it seems boring. Why not dedicate writings to Rhode Island or Hawaii? Doesn't New York generate more sparks for the imagination than Iowa? (I am not prejudiced against Iowa: as a son of the Plains, I spent five of my best youthful years in that state and still savor memories of people who live there.)

I have gone on a bit about this because I want to foreword this book with a takeoff on Robinson and make the claim that the book you are about to read could well have been prefaced with these two words:

"From Iowa"

Professor Everist was born and grew up in Iowa. Her value as an author will soon win your attention and favor. I am moved by a word of José Ortega y Gasset: "Tell me your landscape, and I will tell you who you are." But who we are is by no means exhausted by one geographical reference. Professor

Everist and her husband and children spent two decades in the metropolitan areas of St. Louis, Detroit, and New Haven, Connecticut, most of that time ministering in the inner city, walking the neighborhood, which shaped both her life and her theology. They returned to Iowa, where she has taught many years at Wartburg Theological Seminary in Dubuque, a learning community where students are encouraged to listen deeply not only to Scripture but also to one another.

Professor Everist, a very observant person, gathers into her vision and soul the landscapes in which she has lived. The key to her discernment is a love of and care for people and their stories. She teaches her pastoral and diaconal ministry students to do the same, how to walk with people in their diverse neighborhoods and to listen to their stories in the languages of their daily lives. Their stories and hers, reaching from Iowa across the United States and beyond, become the grist for Everist's narrative art, and she translates that love to people from anywhere. "People from anywhere" make their appearances on many pages; Everist hones her talents, sharpens her vision, and focuses the stories on people especially in various kinds of need. In these accounts we meet passersby whom she—and her students— never pass by. As I read the stories, I kept feeling that I would know on a first-name basis the people who appear here with only a first name after a first-page of readerly acquaintance.

Persons who are graced or are vividly in need of grace—you are one of them—"under God," are the real focus or subjects of this book, but they are special people who experience the grace about which Everist writes so well. They may not always be highly aware of the grace-full existence available to them, or with the promise and potential realization of grace with which she endows them—just as the reader may not have experienced "yet" what the reader will experience upon meeting each in print.

That's how God works, in the Everist vision. I was struck from the first pages and then, through them all, with the "I-Thou" perspective, the personal angle, in a world so often reduced to the "I-It" of mere objects. Just for fun, with the help of the computer's search device, I started counting all the times "we" or "us" showed up, but soon gave up, once the usage of the plural personal pronoun had worked its effect. Again, it's all personal; that's how grace works, whether from God or among the people who respond.

Two more things. First, this is a book of stories. I know, I know: grace is a concept, in its own way also a "thing," to be treated in various ways, including by diverse servants of the word. Professor Everist is a teaching theologian who begins not with Christian dogmatics or religious philosophy but in the world God created and in which ordinary people live. She may be able to impress with abstractions but she finds the challenge in helping people think theologically by beginning with the complexities of daily life and by doing theology together inductively and constructively. She could use words that end with "-ation," as in "justification," "sanctification," or "propitiation," but she would not work her effects with them nearly as well as she does through her stories. (Do we properly recognize the influence of biblical parables on this superbly informed student of the Bible?)

That leaves the other key to this book: it is full of stories. Philosopher Alasdair MacIntyre notes that humans are "storytelling" animals. And somewhere Martin Buber proposed that God created the world because he loved stories and needs a world of people to be part of stories. As tellers of their stories, people conversed and converse with God. Experts on philosophy *and* grammar often note that argument has its purpose in life, but conversation more often opens participants to change. This is clearly a book that bids for conversation, a fact signaled by the many, many questions within the plot and at the end of the chapters. They are invitations to conversations on the life-changing, life-giving reality of divine grace. Let the conversation begin, following through on an author's call from Iowa and into all the world.

Martin E. Marty
Lutheran pastor and Distinguished Service Professor Emeritus
at the University of Chicago

Preface

How can faith speak directly to people's real lives? How can conversation around Scripture make "all the difference" in the arenas of someone's daily world? People who have heard the Bible many times—or for the first time—want to know in the terms and images of their life situation. "When my world seems to be shaking all around me, why doesn't it help to hear 'You are forgiven'?" And ministerial leaders as well as lay people ask, "What can I say to someone who feels totally alienated from God?"

Seventy Images of Grace in the Epistles . . . That Make All the Difference in the World is a book for all who are concerned about the gap between what people hear on Sunday morning—even about what they deeply believe—and what they do in daily life all week long. It is intended to help people make connections and to empower them for their ministries in daily life. We will present the interplay of stories of people's actual lives and Epistle images of grace. This book will neither moralize nor sentimentalize but help people begin to recognize the depth of the human predicament and the power of the gospel, thereby becoming equipped for vocation, not out of guilt, but from freedom.

Why talk about grace in the languages of the arenas of people's daily lives? Aren't the words "justification by grace through faith" Sunday words? Is not faith something I simply apply to my life in the world? Many people think so, leaving theology and deep biblical thought to the clergy. We who are clergy and theologians could be tempted to separate call to faith from call to ministry in daily life. However, we then miss the intricacies of the particular. There are not different kinds of grace, nor different places to live out our faith. God is not detached from the human situations and predicaments in which people are immersed. Jesus Christ's incarnation means he not only put on flesh but entered, and still enters, the places in which we live and work and relate to each other. It is in those places that the gospel meets the world's great need.

We need to be able to name the human predicaments in our daily arenas and hear—and speak—grace there. It is not sufficient to merely try to be good people, or to apply what we heard on Sunday, but all of us, young and old, actually can do theology there. We are transformed by grace in that place, in the languages of daily life, the "vernacular," as Martin Luther put it. Then, through grace in Jesus Christ, all of the baptized, the *laos,* are freed and empowered to be the priesthood of all believers, for ministry in daily life. Therefore we need a broad range of images to meet the broad range of human situations crying out for grace. Scripture itself provides them.

The Images

The church through the centuries has often focused on sin and atonement (or the legal image of forensic justification) as the central way to speak of salvation, but in the Epistles that is not a major image at all. Death/Life and Captive/Free are found much more frequently. If the human problem is death, Jesus Christ has brought new life. If the human problem is bondage, the good news is that Jesus brings freedom. Other major images are Darkness/Light and Alienation/Belonging. All of the baptized, members together of the priesthood of all believers, need to hear the gospel of God's grace in terms of their own specific situations. Theologian Letty Russell wrote that Jesus did not say to the blind person, "You can walk," nor to the person who could not walk, "You can see."[1] Christ met people on the road and asked, "What do you want me to do for you?" Jesus cared about people, the societal problems related to human need, and God's saving justice in the world in which they lived.

There no doubt are more images of grace in the Epistles than I will have enumerated and described here. Likewise, images should not limit. God's work in Christ is beyond any image or metaphor. Readers of the Epistles will make their own discoveries. Any attempt to put concepts in boxes, or to debate them, misses the purpose. These seventy images are arranged in eight chapters, grouped by themes; those images used most frequently have been

1. Letty M. Russell, *Human Liberation in a Feminist Perspective: A Theology* (Philadelphia: Westminster, 1974) 53.

placed at the beginning of each chapter. Minor images, such as Broken Off/ Grafted On to the Tree, follow. We encounter the images in the texts and they encounter us. An index of texts used is provided at the back of the book.

The Stories

The stories in the book are those of real people. Names and situations have been changed as appropriate. To begin where people are is to engage in a ministry of accompaniment. Such ministry requires "walking with" and deep listening. *Together* we discover the human predicament, and, by God's grace, *together* we discern God's good news in Jesus Christ. Sometimes a story introduces an image; sometimes it comes at the end, or at the end of two or three smaller images. Sometimes the story is intertwined with the biblical texts. Often we hear writers, many of whom are former students of Wartburg Theological Seminary, telling in first person the story of the person with whom he or she is walking. The stories presented here are edited excerpts from longer stories written about people living out their vocations in ministry in daily life.

We can start from either direction: the stories of human lives and people hungering for the grace of God, or with a scriptural image. If we begin with the human situation, we cannot simply look for an "answer" in Scripture, in a proof-texting way. Nor should we take one of the images and project it onto someone as though it were a sort of personality test—for example, "Joe is alienation/belonging; Melinda is darkness/light." The goal is to look at and listen to people as we meet them on the road in daily life. Just recently, at a church potluck, a retired professional man said to me, "I'm glad spring is coming, so I can be doing yardwork. During this long winter I have felt so useless." The good news for him was not "You are forgiven," but that in the human predicament of feeling useless, Christ continues to call him with his gifts. (Uselessness/Gifts, we find, is a major image in the Epistles.) We need to listen carefully to people's comments and learn their stories, and to convey in words—more so in action—the good news of Jesus Christ in its many and varied expressions. Each person's story is significant and all of our callings (vocations) are equal in God's sight. This is countercultural in a society marred by income inequality in which people's worth is tied to the compensation they receive for their work. Our calling (our *vocatio*) is rooted in the death and resurrection of Jesus Christ.

Preface

The stories in this book may or may not relate precisely to yours. There is always room for your own stories or stories of people with whom you walk to become part of your reflection and conversation. Stories beget stories and so the conversation continues. Questions for personal reflection and collegial conversations are provided at the end of each image. They also are embedded throughout the text rhetorically, particularly connecting the image to twenty-first-century reality. These questions are not "yes or no," "right or wrong," but rather are meant to draw people in more deeply and to challenge us all for ministry in daily life.

The Readers

This book, while based on solid biblical work, is explicitly written in accessible language rather than the language of the academy. It is intended for a broad readership, including ministerial leaders and all people in the Christian faith community. This book can be read alone but would be more productively used in a group setting such as a pastor's class, an adult study forum, a Bible class, or a peer support group. It could be used as an introduction to Christian faith or as a reintroduction for people considering returning to a faith community after being away for a number of years. A campus ministry setting is another possibility. It could be used in any number of formal educational settings, including seminaries, because students preparing for public ministry often feel intimidated by and not competent to enter into a parishioner's world.

In addition to teaching ministries, this book provides a broad range of images to use in sermon preparation. It heightens our awareness of images not only in the Epistles but also in the Gospels and provides material for thematic preaching. In liturgical planning, the book heightens our awareness of the many images of grace, not only in Scripture but also in hymns and prayers. In pastoral care ministry, or spiritual direction, this book helps pastors, lay care ministers, and spiritual directors listen in the languages people use to describe their lives, meeting people where they are in times of stress and during opportunities for growth.

Blessings as you enter the Letters and become engaged in the many ways God has reached out and continues to reach out with unconditional love in Jesus Christ.

Norma Cook Everist
Wartburg Theological Seminary, Dubuque, Iowa, 2014

Acknowledgments

Because I have been engaged in this work over the years, I have many people to thank, not all of whom are mentioned here. I particularly thank Joe Daiker, Roberta M. Pierce, and Tami Groth, student assistants during the years I was working on compilation and completion of this book. I add my thanks to former student assistants Chris deForest, Gloria Stubitsch, and Katherine Woolf for their faithful collaborative work, and to Nancy Woodin, administrative assistant to the faculty, for her meticulous proofreading. I give my appreciation to my colleague Craig Nessan, with whom I taught as we invited senior seminary students to walk with lay people. I am so pleased that Martin E. Marty agreed to write the Foreword for this book. I have enjoyed working with my editor at Wipf and Stock, Charlie Collier, whose initial interest and consistent support have made all the difference in the world.

I thank the following people for stories about themselves or, in most cases, about their "walking with" a person in daily life: Alicia Anderson, Shannon Arnold, Alyssa Augustson, Matthew T. Barnhouse, Hannah Benedict, Jackie Cook, Trisha DeBoer, Allison deForest, Chris deForest, Christopher Deines, Amanda Esping, Mark Everist, Arnold Flater, Lee R. Gable, Robert Garton, Donald W. Glanzer Jr., Jeremy D. Johnson, Kirsten Curtis, Josh Knudsen, Benjamin Splichal Larson, Jonathan Splichal Larson, Renee Splichal Larson, Joseph L. Liles, Rob Martin, Melinda McVey McCluskey, Ray McKechnie, Rich McLear, Chuck Meyer, D. Patti Meyer, Rich Mohr-Kelly, Roberta M. Pierce, Michael J. Rahlf, Scott Ralston, J. Mamy Ranaivoson, Megan Reedstrom, Malcolm P. Ridgeway Sr., William Rosin, Donna Runge, Arlyn Rusche, Arhiana S. Shek, Emily Lynn Shipman, Rhia Strohm, Gloria Stubitsch, Rod Thompson, Amy Deloach Waelchli, and Andy Zoerb.

Acknowledgments

Now engaged in faithful ministries all over the United States, these people, many of them former students, walked alongside others, listened as they told their stories in the languages of their daily lives, and wrote so that their voices would be heard. The stories have been edited, with permission, to fit the pages of this book. The names of the subjects, places, and authors have been changed as appropriate. The stories are real and also, as Martin Marty wrote, become part of the narrative as "people from anywhere" who are loved by God's grace.

Introduction

1. Human Predicament/Grace

The members of the *laos*, the people of God, carry out their ministries faithfully, sometimes in the midst of struggle, but often the full meaning of the gospel in their lives doesn't seem to fit unless it is in guilt/forgiveness language. What images would relate to the ministries in daily life of people you know? Estranged/Partners? Weakness/Strength? Judgment/Mercy? Futility/Purpose? Death/Life? Division/Unity? Labor/Rest? What are the human problems, challenges, and predicaments they face? What are their "working" theologies? In what ministries in daily life are they already engaged? Are they able to connect biblical and theological concepts with these ministries? The first of the seventy images of grace in the Epistles is presented here in the Introduction as a basis for all the rest.

Steve the Salesperson

Lee walked with Steve, who works full-time as a salesperson at a big-box store in the windows and doors department. Steve said that the fundamental component of his ministry is integrity and trustworthiness. When asked about the effects of sin and human brokenness, he said, "I see it in death and dying." His boss had three significant losses within a few days. "I took his hand between mine and assured him God was with us in all our pain. I could tell he appreciated that." Steve ministers to his boss, but for some reason he doesn't call it ministry. He ministers to customers, too, in certain situations. "I also see human need in my customers—especially the elderly ones. One will come into the store and seem bewildered by the size of the place. Even if she isn't looking for a window or a door, I make sure she finds what she's looking for."

When asked where he might see God's grace at his workplace, Steve responded, "I haven't broken the rules at the store and so I haven't experienced God's grace there." Even though Steve shows God's grace and love to broken people, for him grace is synonymous with forgiveness of certain sins, so he doesn't think he is experiencing it except when he feels condemned for something. Grace is much larger than Steve's conception of it.

What Is the "Human Predicament"? What Is Grace?

So what do we call this human situation? The human condition? Human brokenness? People hungering for the grace of God? I refer to this as the "human predicament," which relates both to the human relationship with God and people's relationships with one another. It is "sin" in the broadest and deepest sense. And this problem is active, not just passive (e.g., "It happened *to* me"). We need to be surrounded by God's unconditional love in Jesus Christ through the body of Christ in order to begin to deal with the radical ramifications of the human predicament. Otherwise, we hide and blame. The human predicament is vertical and horizontal, personal and communal, complex and systemic.

The writers of the Epistles do not mince words in naming the particular human predicaments in the young Christian communities. Here are a few samples: "It has been reported to me by Chloe's people that there are quarrels among you, my brothers and sisters" (1 Cor 1:11); "Some proclaim Christ from envy and rivalry . . ." (Phil 1:15); "You who were once estranged and hostile in mind, doing evil deeds . . ." (Col 1:21);"Recalling your tears, I long to see you . . ." (2 Tim 1:4); ". . . even if now for a little while you have had to suffer various trials . . ." (1 Pet 1:6).

In exploring images of grace, or, one could say, the theology of salvation (soteriology), I mean God's agency in the salvation of humanity through the incarnation, ministry, death, and resurrection of Jesus, the Christ. As we expand our range of salvation images, we can meet people in the many diverse manifestations of the human predicament. The radical grace of God is always a surprise, and always life-changing. Words of grace, almost without exception, begin each letter to the early Christian communities. Here are the beginnings to the Epistles cited above: "To the church of God that is in Corinth, to those who are sanctified in Christ Jesus, called to be saints, together with all those who in every place call on the name of our Lord Jesus Christ, both their Lord and ours: Grace to you and peace from God our Father and the Lord Jesus Christ" (1 Cor 1:2–3); "To all the saints in Christ Jesus who are in Philippi, with the bishop and deacons, Grace to you and peace from God our Father and the Lord Jesus Christ" (Phil 1:1–2); "Grace to you and peace from God our Father. In our prayers for you we always thank God . . ." (Col 1:2–3); "To Timothy, my beloved child: Grace, mercy and peace . . ." (2 Tim 1:2); "May grace and peace be yours in abundance" (1 Pet 1:2).

The good news is for the community; it is not just about "me and Jesus." The Epistle images make it clear that "forgiveness," "life," "reconciliation," and "freedom," among other concepts, are plural and so meant for communal life in Christ. This new life together is unachievable and unattainable on our own. The gospel is a gift. Dietrich Bonhoeffer knew the dangers of being the church in a dangerous world. He also wrote about the great loneliness in community. We make demands on one another. We fail to hear the other's cries of pain. As the love of God restores communion between God and humans in Christ, so too the human community is transformed into a living reality of love. The Holy Spirit makes us aware of the ways in which we are estranged from one another so that we know we need Christ. The Spirit places us within the divine community so that members of the community no longer see one another as claim (demand) but as gift.[2]

- How do you see the human predicament in the arenas of your daily life? How is the human predicament both personal and communal? Complex and systemic? Who is hurting? How are relationships with God and with one another affected?

- What is the word of grace that would be good news for you on a Tuesday afternoon or a Thursday morning? Jesus who reconciles? Christ who provides a firm foundation? God who through grace creates community and belonging where there is alienation? What other image might you use for grace?

2. Dietrich Bonhoeffer, *The Communion of Saints,* trans. James Schaef (New York: Harper and Row, 1960) 106–20.

Introduction

The Epistles and the Encounter

The Epistles are often underutilized in faith communities. And sometimes we find their words less than helpful, such as when the writers, in their context, do not criticize the oppressive systems of slavery and male domination. However, just as leaders in the young churches were engaged with the challenge of the relevancy of the gospel in the lives of individual Christians and congregations, so we, too, face that challenge now. What systemic, oppressive systems need to be addressed today?

There are many books about the historical backgrounds and contexts of the Epistles. Readers will have no difficulty finding a vast number from which to choose to study. Here we take a different approach, exploring each image across the Epistles. At times this may seem frustratingly like looking at a Scripture passage out of context. True. This searching for use of images is like doing a word study across Scripture, not as a substitute for but as a complement to deep study of each Epistle itself.

Paul S. Minear's work has long inspired my own, particularly his *Images of the Church in the New Testament*, published in 1960.[3] My work in this book differs from Minear's in that I am using only the Epistles, not the Gospels. I echo some of Minear's statements about scope and method in explaining my biblical research and use of the Epistles.

- The New Testament is full of images of the work of Christ beyond Sin/ Guilt and forgiveness.

- In my venture I am not pursuing the history of these images toward their origins in the ancient world. Nor am I carrying these images forward, pursuing their use in subsequent centuries in the church.

- I am not exploring the topic of whether there is unity of perspective within the New Testament, nor even within the Epistles, given the varied locations and times of writing. Each community had its own challenges and each letter its own integrity.

- I am very aware that there are huge differences in the thought world of the first-century church and the twenty-first-century church, as well

---

3. Paul S. Minear, *Images of the Church in the New Testament* (Philadelphia: Westminster, 1960) 11. This book was the result of a work assigned to him by the Theological Communion on Christ and the Church, established by the Faith and Order Department of the World Council of Churches in 1954.

as significant global, cultural, and language differences within this twenty-first-century church.[4]

- I use the term *image* to refer also to metaphor and figurative expressions. In distinction from Minear's work, some of my "images" are descriptions of actual human situations, needing no metaphor.

- Soteriological images of the human predicament and gospel action often are inseparable from the new life of the Christian. Although I looked specifically at soteriology, when images of the new life were organically connected, I included them.

- I frequently use only part of a verse in lifting up a particular image. Ellipses are used and punctuation is adapted for ease of reading. A verse is referenced in the whole rather than just in part—for example, v. 3 not v. 3b. Likewise the reference may include more verses than directly quoted, verses that also enlighten the image.

- The reader always is encouraged to read the context for further insights.

Minear conservatively estimated that there are more than eighty images of the church in the New Testament, the number easily being increased to one hundred if the various Greek words were counted separately.[5] Since I am using only the Epistles, I hesitate to estimate the exact number of images of soteriology in the New Testament, or even in the Epistles themselves. Giving a definitive number would be misleading. Simply counting is not the objective. My goal is to expand our concepts, to open up the many ways we can speak about God's work in Jesus Christ that meets us in our human predicament. Minear, at the conclusion of his work, questioned the division between major and minor images, even though he had arranged his book that way. A minor image, one used less frequently, may give no less an authentic expression: "Nor can we measure significance or authenticity by the number of appearances of the image or by the number of authors who use it."[6]

---

4. Ibid, 14–18.
5. Ibid., 28.
6. Ibid., 252.

Introduction

Intertwined Images

The images of God's saving work in Christ Jesus are sometimes intertwined. For example in Col 1:13 we have God's *rescue,* the image of *darkness,* and the terms *redemption* and *forgiveness of sins.* All pertain—Christ's work is comprehensive. This may make our point even more strongly, for at any one time in a given person's life, one of those images may speak more powerfully than another. Likewise one does not separate the work of Christ from the image of Christ. For example, in Col 1:15–18 Christ is described as "the image of the invisible God," "the firstborn of all creation," "the head of the body, the church," and "the firstborn from the dead." Each image presents Jesus differently, empowering people for their own vocations in Christ.

Guides for Engagement

At the end of the book, guides for engagement will provide specific, concrete suggestions on how the book can be used to make a difference in daily life.

Learning Together

This guide will help with setting and maintaining a healthy learning environment in which people may engage each other at their own comfort level. We will explore various settings and methods for teaching and learning in these settings as well as ways to lead conversational discussion fruitfully.

Using an Image

People may look at each image and ask, "How does this image speak to me?" Or they may consider a friend, family member, or parishioner and think, "How does this image help me relate the gospel to this person, whose life situation cries out for good news?" This guide will provide multiple ways to use these images in ministry.

Introduction

Walking With

Rather than using surveys or interviews conducted in the fellowship hall, this guide helps do actual walks with people in the arenas of their daily vocations. There will be suggestions on how to enter the real worlds of parishioners and walk with them, listening not only to their stories but also to the images they use and to the challenges they face.

Listening in the Language of the Other

In pastoral care, or peer support groups, the focus will be to listen for the human predicament in the other person's story. The goal is to help people discover images that name their own experiences. Throughout the book readers will encounter the various ways people speak in the languages of their many arenas of daily life.

Discerning Vocations

This guide will help people think about not just "choosing a job" but how to explore vocation throughout the life cycle. The challenges are great and the disappointments real. The goal is to grow in ways to help each other in the Christian community listen, support, and discern vocation in order to make a difference in the world.

CHAPTER 1

From Bondage to Freedom

Christ leads us from bondage to freedom through his death and resurrection. Captivity/Freedom is a major image of grace in the Epistles. We have been set free from the bondage of sin, which changes our lives in personal and communal, private and public ways. Even while living in various kinds of bondages, we are no longer slaves, but free to serve. A less frequently used but significant image is Illegal/Legal. We do not need to pass God's laws. Neither are we now divided by human designations of law-abiding and "illegal" people. Sin/Forgiveness is an image of grace used very frequently in the church, but it is not a uniquely major image in the Epistles. Forgiveness is important, of course, because it gives us the power to live freely with God and with one another.

Christ, as sacrifice and high priest, frees us from living under the old covenant to being part of a new covenant and for new opportunities for ministry. A minor image that may speak powerfully to some is Fire/Snatched from Fire. Likewise, being Engulfed in Human Problems/Having an Advocate is the word of grace that will set people free from the oppressive complexities of life. The final image of bondage in this chapter is Weight of Sin/Weight Lifted. Christ has lifted that weight. This image, like the others, moves us from bondage to freedom. Let's begin!

2. Captivity/Freedom

"Grace to you and peace from God our Father and the Lord Jesus Christ, who gave himself for our sins to set us free . . ." (Gal 1:3–4). We begin with a major image of grace in the Epistles: Captivity/Freedom. One could isolate this image to past societal sins of slavery; however, that would be to ignore the fact that there may be more people enslaved today (e.g., sex trafficking) than at any time in history. In addition, there are many kinds of captivity in the human experience. The image of Captivity/Freedom is found frequently in the Pauline Epistles. In Eph 4:8, grace is expressed as Christ, when he ascended, making "captivity itself captive."[1]

There are many references to the imprisonment of Paul and others (Phil 1:12ff.), often telling how they see their imprisonment as actually helping to spread the gospel. In Colossians: "pray for us as well that God will open to us a door for the word, that we may declare the mystery of Christ, for which I am in prison . . ." (Col 4:3). We are to "remember those who are in prison, as though you were in prison with them; those who are being tortured, as though you yourselves were being tortured" (Heb 13:3). Bondage is real and is deeply connected to the work of Christ.

Malcolm's Letters from Prison

"Greetings in the name of our Lord and Savior Jesus Christ. I pray this finds you well and in very good health and Spirit."[2] From 1981 to 1991, and again from 1998 to the present, I have been blessed to have been corresponding with Malcolm, who has been incarcerated all that time. (Our family has known him and his family since he was a young teenager.) I have pages and pages of handwritten letters, filling four file folders.

He began his letter of July 25, 1998, by saying,

> Blessed be the God and Father of our Lord Jesus Christ who has blessed us with all spiritual blessings in the heavenly place. I hope and pray that this letter arrives to find you in the very best of God's tender loving care. I am doing well. My wounds have just about all healed and I am dealing with forgiving those who tried to take my life for I know that my ministry will never reach its fullest potential without total forgiveness on my part. I lead a strong men's group

1. Reference Ps 68:18.
2. The opening of Malcolm's letter of July 10, 2000.

here. The men are really hungry not only for the Word but also to know God in a more personal and powerful way. I don't want to do any more incarcerated time, but I have to be strong. I look forward to your correspondence and words of encouragement.

Malcolm is repentant of his crime. His letter of January 1, 2000: "Our faith community is growing in here. God knows the restraints that we face. I've been taking a more active role in the services. I don't feel comfortable anymore just sitting back and observing. I haven't spoken at a service yet, but I stay prepared for when the opportunity arises. I know I have to live a life that is indicative of who I am inside and I hope that will lead others to Christ."

Through the years his letters tell of the real-life struggles of the pain of absence from his family, particularly when he is suddenly moved from one prison to another. He is now some four hundred miles away from home. But his letters are full of hope and the gospel. I consider him a kind of St. Paul sending epistles. He is imprisoned but free to serve in his particular "ministry in daily life," proclaiming the good news of Jesus to the men where he is, teaching, often counseling the younger men as they come in, offering guidance. In recent years he has been working with a program that prepares men for life beyond prison walls even though his own sentence may not end soon.

The Many Dimensions of Bondage

In the book of Romans, the Captivity/Freedom image is prominent. "We know that our old self was crucified with him so the body of sin might be destroyed, and we might no longer be enslaved to sin. For whoever has died is freed from sin" (6:6–7). This concept is expanded in 6:17–23. It is repeated, "having once been slaves of sin . . ." (v. 17); "having been set free from sin, [you] have become slaves of righteousness" (v. 18). Also, "you once presented your members as slaves to impurity . . . so now present your members as slaves to righteousness for sanctification" (v. 19). Having been "freed from sin and enslaved to God" (6:22), we are now "dead to that which held us captive" (7:6). Paul says he was "sold into slavery under sin" (7:14). And although the freedom one has in Christ is now certain, the struggle goes on: "I see in my members another law at war with the law of my mind, making me captive to the law of sin that dwells in my members" (7:23). The good news for all these kinds of captivity is that "the law of the Spirit of life in Christ Jesus has set you free from the law of sin and of death" (8:2).

"Before faith came, we were imprisoned and guarded under the law . . ." (Gal 3:23). We were "enslaved to the elemental spirits of the world" (Gal 4:3). We are free from sin because Christ himself "bore our sin in his body on the cross so that, free from sins, we might live for righteousness" (1 Pet 2:24).

Being freed in Christ changes our lives and relationships, to God and to other human beings, in both private and public ways. Examples: "You are no longer a slave but a child, and if a child, then also an heir, through God" (Gal 4:7); "We ourselves were once . . . slaves to various passions and pleasures . . ." (Titus 3:3); "See to it that no one takes you captive through philosophy and empty deceit, according to human tradition, according to the elemental spirits of the universe, and not according to Christ" (Col 2:8); "For freedom Christ has set us free. Stand firm, therefore, and do not submit again to a yoke of slavery" (Gal 5:1).

The letter of Paul to Philemon is about the change in relationship that comes to us through Christ. Onesimus is a slave, but Paul speaks of himself as a prisoner of Christ Jesus. Onesimus has become a Christian; Paul sends him back to Philemon, but "no longer as a slave but more than a slave, a beloved brother" (v. 16). In the New Testament world, slavery was an accepted reality; however, freedom in Christ transcended institutional bondage: "Whatever good we do, we will receive the same again from the Lord, whether we are slaves or free" (Eph 6:8). Freedom in Christ transcends and transforms human bondage, oppression, and divisions: ". . . there is no longer slave or free . . ." (Gal 3:28).

Being captive is broadened if one includes other words—for example, being "trapped" by "many senseless and harmful desires that plunge people into ruin and destruction" (1 Tim 6:9). Likewise, the Epistles use the image of enslavement in terms of false prophets, who "promise freedom" but who themselves "are slaves of corruption: for people are slaves to whatever masters them" (2 Pet 2:19). They may have escaped the defilements of the world through the knowledge of our Lord and Savior Jesus Christ, but they "are again entangled in them and overpowered," and thus "the last state has become worse for them than the first" (2 Pet 2:20).

Freedom for Service

This new liberty is a gift and is to be used in service. Malcolm, while in prison, uses his liberty in service to fellow inmates. In a recent letter to him, I wrote, "I liked hearing about your Weekend Walk with Jesus and the themes of discovery, spirituality and action. And forty-two men taking the walk!"

Struggles continue, however. The outside world's entanglements with systemic injustice permeate prisons, too. His letter of August 12, 2013:

> I continue to be busy as ever here. With the George Zimmerman verdict, racial tensions have been high. People talk about our country making huge leaps in terms of racial equality but nothing could be further from the truth. Especially in the criminal justice system. The new Jim Crow is in full effect.[3] Young blacks (and us older men as well) are growing sick and tired of being the targets of murder and injustice. How do you teach these youngsters conflict resolution when every time you look around, one of them is being murdered and no one is held accountable? We teach and expect them to resolve disputes in a peaceful manner, but that is not what is being done to them.

In a letter dated November 9, 2013: "Our country is quickly evolving into a have and have-not society." He adds in the same letter, "I am able to teach some classes and in the process God will draw men to Jesus. Your words give me strength. I know that God is the God of justice and grace and love and compassion and hope. It is because of God's compassion that we are not consumed."

Malcolm's letters sometimes show his wit as well as his commitment to ministry within prison walls. He wrote, in the summer of 2012,

> How's my sister doing this fine day? It's hot here. I can see on the weather it's even hotter where you are. I've been praying for those states hit with the fires. My heart goes out to them. I received your letter and the kind and encouraging words from my brothers and sisters, your students. They always seem to come at a time when I need them most. We have a saying here, "Every sentence must come to an end." I believe that is true, but this has been a long run-on sentence thus far. I keep coming to commas instead of a period. In spite of it my hope is in the Lord.
>
> I am in the tenth week of teaching my "Men Concerned with Youth, Family and Friends" class. Like you, I get my greatest joy and inspiration when I am in front of a classroom. The program in Chicago, "Ceasefire" and "Chance for Life" in Detroit use men who have been in prison who are trained in mediation and conflict

---

3. See Michelle Alexander, *The New Jim Crow: Mass Incarceration in the Age of Color-blindness* (New York: New Press, 2012): "We have not ended racial caste in America; we have merely redesigned it" (2).

resolution in neighborhoods to make a difference. I don't know where the Lord is taking me in all of this. I just continue to feel called and ask God to use me. I'm in a situation I can't do anything about so I pray every day that God will shape and use my life.

And in a recent letter:

Dear Norma,

I pray that all is well with you and the rest of the family. It's been a while since I wrote. I honestly don't know where the time goes. As fast as it flies by it still doesn't go fast enough. I'm teaching cognitive thinking and that gives me the opportunity to still breathe on small groups at a time. It has become my mission to reach as many as I can. I know that it's because of God's grace and strength that I keep moving forward. I read your letters and feel the connection that we are a part of the same body of Christ. Jesus is the tie that binds. Take care of yourself and give my love to the rest of the family. Malcolm.

How do we use our liberty, even while yet not totally free? "Take care that this liberty of yours does not somehow become a stumbling block to the weak" (1 Cor 8:9). Paul, in 1 Cor 9, talks about himself in asking rhetorically, "Am I not free?" (v. 1). Do we not have rights? What are those rights resulting in being free in Christ? "Though I am free with respect to all, I have made myself a slave to all, so that I might win more of them" (v. 19). He does all for the sake of the gospel (v. 23). The gospel is the measure of how to use this freedom. "As servants of God, live as free people, yet do not use your freedom as a pretext for evil" (1 Pet 2:16). Rather, "You were called to freedom, brothers and sisters. . . . Through love, become slaves to one another" (Gal 5:13).[4]

The Letter to the Hebrews is explicit that through death Christ destroyed the one who had the power of death and so freed "those who all their lives were held in slavery by the fear of death" (2:15). And finally, "Where the Spirit of the Lord is, there is freedom" (2 Cor 3:17).

- Consider the many millions of people who have been enslaved throughout history and those who are enslaved today. What is our calling to set the captive free?

---

4. See Martin Luther, "A Treatise on Christian Liberty," in *Three Treatises* (Philadelphia: Muhlenberg, 1947) 251: "A Christian is a perfectly free lord of all, subject to none. A Christian is a perfectly dutiful servant of all, subject to all."

- In what ways do you or the people you love live in various forms of bondage? What does the freedom of the gospel of Jesus Christ mean for your life, now and forever?

- How does grace, freedom from bondage, have the power to transform relationships personally, communally, and globally?

3. Illegal/Legal

Freedom from bondage to the religious law, from being saved "by the law," was part of the previous image. Many Christians may use the word *grace*, or even say, "We are saved by grace though faith," but cling to having to prove they are worthy enough to pass God's laws, or to "not break God's law." Grace in Christ means that we are now and always "legal."

In Colossians we hear, "Do not let anyone condemn you," and "Do not let anyone disqualify you . . ." (2:16, 18). God forgave us in Christ Jesus, "erasing the record that stood against us with its legal demands" (Col 2:14). And in Romans we read, "There is therefore now no condemnation for those who are in Christ Jesus" (8:1).

It is so convenient for people to define others as "law-abiding" or "lawbreakers," even giving some the name "illegals." In Romans it is clear that God alone, "through Jesus Christ, will judge the secret thoughts of all" (2:16). God does not name some people "legals" and others "illegals." God has dealt with the law by sending Jesus Christ, thus condemning sin, "so that the just requirements of the law might be fulfilled in us, who walk not according to the flesh but according to the Spirit" (Rom 8:3–4). Does that mean that we should have no civil laws? Of course not, but they do not define a person in God's sight, nor should they define a person's humanity. "Christ is the end of the law so that there may be righteousness for everyone who believes" (Rom 10:4), and further, "Sin will have no dominion over you, since you are not under law but under grace" (Rom 6:14). This transformation through Christ turns things around so that now "love is the fulfilling of the law" (Rom 13:10).

Maria the "Illegal"

The phone call to the United States brought good news. Maria's visa application had finally been accepted. She had been back in Mexico for more than six months—waiting, filling out document after document, waiting still more, uncertain of the outcome. She had staked everything on it.

Twelve years before, Maria, her husband at the time, and their infant daughter had flown to the United States with passports and visas, but, as happens to many immigrants, someone had figured out they were new arrivals and they were robbed for their passports. Unlike U.S. citizens, they were understandably afraid to go to local authorities to report the theft. They lived for nine years in the United States as undocumented. The minute you overstay your visa, you are "illegal."

For all these years, she had lived in Arizona, working, giving birth to a second child—a son—and then going through the breakup of her marriage. Her son and daughter thrived in this country, yet being an illegal was not easy. Maria could not help feeling drawn back to her family in Mexico, where she would have a job, would be free from questions about papers, and would not have to worry about illegality. Finally, she did go back to Mexico. She reported the theft of her passport there. She tried the schools in her city, but her children were miserable; they didn't fit into that culture now, particularly her son, who was born in the United States. Maria determined that her children needed a life in the United States. She sent her children ahead, her daughter with her Mexican passport and her son with his U.S. passport. Maria had no papers, so this time she walked across illegally. It was not just an illegal act; she herself was "illegal."

Back in the United States, she gave birth to another daughter. Life was complex, but of one thing she was sure: she did not want to hide anymore. And she did not want to cross illegally again. So she returned to Mexico with all three children. She would apply for legal status, which would require asking for a pardon, paying a fine, and waiting. She had her children with her, and it would be tempting to keep them in Mexico while she waited. But as the months went on and fall came, she sent them back to the United States so that they could attend school there, in the care of their fathers—one of whom was legal, the other not. She sent her own mother along to help care for them. And so she waited, not knowing if they would ever be more than a border family of "legals" and "illegals." Until that letter came. She had been approved; she would receive a legal visa. She could come, this time not on foot, crossing the desert, but by airplane—legally, crossing with papers, not in the shadows.

Illegal has become a name for Maria, for whole families, for entire communities of people. Illegal immigrants. Illegal "aliens." Laws are laws.

People are people. What is the gospel here? Requirements of the law need to be met. Illegalities will not just magically disappear. They are in need of reform. The issues in individual lives, within extended and divided families, are complex, as are contemporary issues of immigration. However, even though one may yet be "illegal," that one is legal in Christ, who bore the condemnation for us, for all, no matter what borders human beings erect.

- Do you continue to feel that you are under God's law, being judged "good" or "bad," maybe even a "good or bad Christian" by keeping or not keeping certain laws? Do others you know feel this way? What does grace really mean?

- How do we view people according to human-made laws? Have you ever been a "lawbreaker" and so excluded? Have any members of your family, or your friends? How does living in God's grace have the potential to change human relationships and make us agents of change in society?

4. Sin/Forgiveness

This, of course, is the most familiar and perhaps most widely used soteriological image; however, the number of passages that contain it is not overwhelming. In Ephesians we read that we have "redemption through his blood, the forgiveness of our trespasses" (1:7) and "redemption as God's own people" (1:14). Note the use of the plural. Forgiveness is not simply about personal salvation. In 1 Tim 2:3–4 we see that God, our Savior, "desires everyone to be saved." Titus and others show the sinful condition of humankind (e.g., Titus 3:1–3). In Col 1:14 we have the beloved Son "in whom we have redemption, the forgiveness of sins." And 1 Tim 1:15 affirms, "The saying is sure and worthy of full acceptance, that Christ Jesus came into the world to save sinners—of whom I am foremost." In Christ we have "forgiveness of our trespasses," according to the riches of God's grace (Eph 1:7).

In 1 Cor 15:3–4 Christ's work is described: "Christ died for our sins in accordance with the scriptures, and . . . was buried, and . . . was raised on the third day." This work is once and for all, and also ongoing. It is the good news, "through which also you are being saved" (1 Cor 15:2). According to Hebrews, where there is forgiveness of sins, "there is no longer any offering for sin" (Heb 10:18). This forgiveness is not simply a pronouncement of personal salvation in heaven. In 2 Cor 2:5–10, young Christians are urged to forgive when someone has caused pain. "Anyone whom you forgive, I also forgive.

What I have forgiven, if I have forgiven anything, has been for your sake in the presence of Christ" (v. 10). Another important verse concerning forgiveness enjoins Christians to "be kind to one another, tenderhearted, forgiving one another as God in Christ has forgiven you" (Eph 4:32).

Romans, of course, has the most verses using this image. Guilt for sin is not just about bad actions. Both Jews and Greeks are under the *power* of sin and guilt (3:9), but "blessed are those whose iniquities are forgiven and whose sins are covered" (4:7).[5] "There is no distinction, since all have sinned and fall short of the glory of God; they are now justified by God's grace as a gift, through the redemption that is in Christ Jesus" (3:22–24). Then we have the core verses of Romans 5: "Therefore, since we are justified by faith, we have peace with God through our Lord Jesus Christ" (v. 1), and "while we still were sinners Christ died for us" (v. 8). We see again the power of sin at the end of the chapter: "the trespass multiplied" when the law "came in" and where sin exercised dominion. And yet, "where sin increased, grace abounded all the more." Grace exercised "dominion through justification leading to eternal life through Jesus Christ our Lord" (5:20–21). Therefore, we are to let sin exercise no more dominion (6:12): "For sin will have no dominion over you, since you are not under the law but under grace" (6:14).

If we know we have already been forgiven in Jesus Christ, we are more likely to be ready to confess our sins. "Anyone who has committed sins will be forgiven. Therefore confess your sins to one another . . ." (Jas 5:15–16). Still, we are tempted to say we have not been a sinner: "If we say that we have no sin, we deceive ourselves, and the truth is not in us. If we confess our sins, he who is faithful and just will forgive us our sins . . ." (1 John 1:9). In Christ "there is no sin" (1 John 3:5), and John gives further assurance, saying, "I am writing to you, little children, because your sins are forgiven on account of his name" (1 John 2:12). Sin is a significant image of the human predicament, particularly because of the power (dominion) it can have. Jesus Christ has brought forgiveness. The certainty and security is ours for living and serving.

Donald's Need for Forgiveness

Jason listened closely to Donald and tells his story: "Donald told me about how drought had forced him to give up his family farm. He feels persecuted

5. Quoting Ps 32:1

due to federal regulations; the corporate farms are making it impossible to stay competitive. He took me for a tour of what used to be his land and told me stories of growing up and of the importance of tradition, family time, and Sunday worship. He then took me to see his new occupation, driving a truck to pick up glass bottles for a local company. He said that the pay was good, but being on the road all the time was tough. We then drove around the city and he pointed out businesses that had closed. Businesses his friends used to own. I asked him what had happened. He informed me that the little guy can't compete with big business. 'They move in and take over. We either work for them, or move,' he answered.

"After the tour, we went to his house where his wife, Kris, had lunch waiting for us. As we ate, I asked him to tell me about his family. He said it is really hard. 'I mean, everything has been the same around here since I was a boy. Heck, maybe even many years before that. The same neighbors, the same people I see at church every Sunday, and the same businesses handed down from father to son. But now it's all different.' He explained that the older generation is dying off, only now, they don't have anything to pass on to their kids. He believed that was the reason all the young people were leaving the church and the community. 'They don't have any reason to stay here because there is nothing left for them. So they look for something better.' He said he thought that was why his daughter left. There was no farm left to pass on. 'Now she lives so far away, I almost never get to see her. And I have spent more time talking with my granddaughter on Skype than getting to have her sit on my lap or play house with.'

"We spent the better part of the afternoon with him telling stories. I told him that it is why his story matters. I pointed out that his life and traditions were formed by people who had gone before him, and now he is the holder of the stories and history for those still to come.

"Donald was not only grieving but feeling guilty by blaming himself for the loss of his farm, his inability to hand the business on to his daughter, and her leaving to go to the city to find a better life. But he had found a measure of forgiveness through the sharing of story and tradition through his church and community. He is also starting to grasp that many of his friends had faced similar situations and that he may simply be holding on to his personal feeling of sin. His blaming federal regulations and big corporations keeps him in bondage. He is still struggling, but I believe he is starting to understand that his daughter's leaving was out of his control.

"I believe there is a need here for Donald to feel God's love and forgiveness. He needs continued care from the community and to find joy in his new role in life. Through Christ's living word and the power of the cross and resurrection, Donald can find reconciliation with himself and those around him."

- How do you see sin, in all of its complexity? How does the world view sin? Sinners?

- What does forgiveness in the cross and resurrection of Jesus Christ mean for you? For the world?

- How does forgiveness free us to acknowledge our sin and turn from it?

5. Old Covenant/New Covenant

In the Letter to the Hebrews, Christ is the sacrifice and the high priest. He is the "mediator of a new covenant, so that all who are called may receive the promised eternal inheritance, because a death has occurred that redeems them from the transgressions under the first covenant" (9:15).

The writer goes on to compare a covenant to a will, which takes effect only upon the death of the one who made it. In the first covenant there was blood involved—the blood of calves and goats, which Moses sprinkled upon the scroll of the law and the people, saying, "This is the blood of the covenant that God has ordained for you" (9:17–20). The writer points out that almost everything was purified with blood, and without it there was no forgiveness of sins (9:21–22).

This new covenant has made the first covenant "old" and "obsolete." Now, in the new covenant, Christ offered himself as the sacrifice, once for all to remove sin. He sacrificed himself to bear the sins of many and for the forgiveness of all, the final freedom from sin (9:23–28). Jesus "became the guarantee of a better covenant" (7:22). "Jesus has now obtained a more excellent ministry, and to that degree he is the mediator of a better covenant, which has been enacted through better promises. For if that first covenant had been faultless, there would have been no need to look for a second one" (8:6–7). "In speaking of 'a new covenant,' [God] has made the first one obsolete. And what is obsolete and growing old will soon disappear" (8:13).

This image is not entirely limited to Hebrews. In 2 Corinthians the "reading of the old covenant" is like a veil that is set aside only in Christ (3:14). More significantly, knowing that we are not competent in ourselves, we are assured that our competence comes from God, "who has made us competent to be ministers of a new covenant, not of letter but of spirit;" (3:5–6). This image is fundamental to ministry and is present each time we partake of the Eucharist. This is a strong reminder of the grace of God in Christ Jesus: "This cup is the new covenant in my blood. Do this, as often as you drink it, in remembrance of me" (1 Cor 11:25).

Hebrews draws to a close with the blessing, "Now may the God of peace, who brought back from the dead our Lord Jesus, the great shepherd of the sheep, by the blood of the eternal covenant, make you complete in everything good . . ." (Heb 13:20).

Larry: Ministering in Covenantal Relationships

Jack spends a day with Larry and relates this story: "Larry has been married to Debbie, his high school sweetheart, just under two years, and they are expecting their first child in four months. This is his first year as a kindergarten teacher in the city across the river. They just moved into a larger rental house this week. Debbie's brother, Reggie, lives with them in a 'bachelor pad' garage. And sometimes George, her father, a recovering and relapsing alcoholic, stays in the apartment, too, sleeping on the couch.

"I arrived at their home early, around 5:15 a.m., to meet up with Larry and Reggie. Since Reggie doesn't have a car, Larry takes on the responsibility of driving Reggie the fifteen minutes to work each morning. All three of us piled into the car at 5:30 to make sure Reggie arrived at work by 5:45. I sat in the back. After a short conversation between Larry and Reggie about Sunday's pro football game, the car ride was steeped in silence.

"Upon dropping Reggie off, Larry turned to me and said, 'Here's the issue: I could now spend 15 minutes driving back home and attempt to fall back asleep for 30 to 45 minutes, or I could go to the school where I teach, sleep in the parking lot, or sleep in the classroom. Normally I sleep in the classroom, but since you are here we will just sleep in the car.' Upon arriving at the school we slept for an hour, in the car, in the parking lot.

"Waking up to the sound of the cars of other teachers put a hop into Larry's step. We walked into Larry's classroom and I was immediately amazed by the wealth of artwork and projects that adorned the walls, ceiling, and floors. Larry explained that the children's favorite time of day is their craft time and that every child always receives a space to display their work.

"As the children arrived, Larry's demeanor changed completely. I saw an energetic, emotionally engaged, compassionate, and playful Larry as opposed to the overly tired, going-through-the-motions Larry I had seen earlier that morning. He was concerned about the well-being and happiness of every child, and that was evident in his conversation and attentiveness to each child's needs. Larry's role is not without its challenges; three or four of the children consistently disrupt the learning environment of the other students. Larry has a tone and character that he embodies when dealing with these children. He is stern, yet not frightening, relating to them in such a manner that the children examine their own actions and offer solutions or apologies, depending upon the situation."

"Walking with" Larry from the moment his day began enabled Jack to see him in the complexity of his vocation. While Larry understands and accepts his roles, he also sometimes feels captive. He, like so many others, is making sacrifices. He is "doing all he can" and needs to be assured that Christ offered himself as a sacrifice once for all. The good news is that we do not live under the old covenant, whereby blood sacrifices were necessary. We are not called to unending sacrifice. Our competence, even in the midst of pressures, comes from God, who has made us ministers of a new covenant—freeing us, in our many ministries, to a new covenantal relationship with God and with one another.

- We make covenants and contracts and wills all the time. And sometimes we break them. How have such covenants been helpful or harmful in your life?

- How does being embraced by the grace of the new covenant in Christ Jesus ground us for making, keeping, and living in new covenantal relationships with God and with one another?

6. Fire/Snatched from Fire

The Epistle of James uses the image of fire: "How great a forest is set ablaze by a small fire" (3:5). Many have experienced the ravages of fire; some the horror of a forest fire burning out of control. Is there an escape route? Who will put it out or bring it under control? But the letter goes on: "And the tongue is a fire. The tongue is placed among our members as a world of iniquity; it stains the whole body, sets on fire the cycle of nature, and is itself set on fire by hell" (3:6). Ah, who of us has not experienced the human predicament of a community "on fire" because of envy and selfish ambition and false truth? The community itself is in a hellish situation.

I know of an elderly woman whose town was hit by an F5 tornado. Her home was crushed. She escaped only by huddling in the bathroom in the basement. She survived that tragedy, but a few years later the church of which she had been a member for decades experienced the fire of controversy, which burned people and families deeply and finally ended in division. As she neared death, she shared that losing her church was more damaging to her even than losing her home. The tongue is a fire.

Later in James we encounter an equally devastating image: "Come now, you rich people, weep and wail for the miseries that are coming to you. Your riches have rotted, and your clothes are moth-eaten. Your gold and silver have rusted, and their rust will be evidence again you, and it will eat your flesh like fire" (5:1–3). A horrible image. And in Hebrews we read, "Our God is a consuming fire" (12:29). A strong image, not to be used lightly, nor thrown at people in a "fire and brimstone" sermon. However, if people have experienced or are experiencing the realities of fire, literally or as James uses it, the good news that will meet them needs to be just as strong: God has snatched you from the fire in Jesus Christ.

Jude uses this term in writing about the last times. In the midst of divisions, he writes, "But you, beloved, build yourselves up on your most holy faith; pray in the Holy Spirit; keep yourselves in the love of God; look forward to the mercy of our Lord Jesus Christ that leads to eternal life. And have mercy on some who are wavering; save others by snatching them out of the fire . . ." (Jude 20–23).

- Fire is, of course, a good gift needed for heat, cooking food, and more; however, fire can as easily be harmful, even destructive. Have you ever experienced the ravages of fire out of control, damaging all around? Ponder or tell of your experience.

- How have you experienced or seen the damage the "tongue as a fire" can do in the midst of human community? What have you felt? Have you seen Christ at work, snatching people from that fire? How might we be part of the working of grace in the midst of such fires?

7. Engulfed in Problems/Having an Advocate

"What then are we to say about these things? If God is for us, who is against us?" (Rom 8:31). Who of us does not need someone on our side? Who of us is not in need of an advocate at some point in our professional, public, or personal life? Christ is not only savior and redeemer but also advocate. God is on our side. Paul goes on, saying that if God did not withhold God's own Son, but gave Christ up for all of us, will not God also give us everything else? Who, therefore, can bring—or prevail in—any charge against us? (Rom 8:32–33) We who are engulfed in sinning and in the problem of sin itself have an advocate who intercedes for us: "Who is to condemn? It is Christ Jesus, who died, yes, who was raised, who is at the right hand of God, who indeed intercedes for us" (Rom 8:34).

First John uses these words to comfort: "My little children, I am writing these things to you so that you may not sin. But if anyone does sin, we have an advocate with the Father, Jesus Christ the righteous" (1 John 2:1). Hebrews likewise uses this image of Christ as an advocate who intercedes, not only once but continuously: Christ "is able for all time to save those who approach God through him, since he always lives to make intercession for them" (7:25). We have an advocate, and not just once—Christ advocates for our freedom again and again, so that there is no possibility of our being engulfed in sin with no hope of escape.

This, of course, is not so for many people in this world, whose lives are engulfed in sin (sometimes systemic sin that is not of their own doing), in poverty, in addiction, in the criminal justice system, or in debt. We all participate in the bondage of being engulfed in these problems. Often people are left alone, with systems arrayed against them. At just such times, to know that grace is having Jesus Christ as the sure, certain, and constant advocate makes all the difference in the world.

- When have you or someone you care about needed an advocate? What were the circumstances? What were the outcomes?

- Ponder Christ as your ongoing advocate. How does, or could, that make a difference in your daily life?

Natasha and Erin: Advocates for Each Other

Jeanette, who walked with and listened carefully to Natasha and Erin, tells this story: "Four months ago Natasha had a job at McDonald's, but for reasons beyond her control, she was asked to leave and has not been able to find another job since. She is a single mom of three-year-old Jason. At times, feelings of desperation and helplessness threaten to overcome her. Then she remembers she is not alone. For the last year Natasha and her son have been living with her friend, Erin, and Erin's seven-year-old daughter, Kristin. Erin has provided the home and Natasha has been a support and advocate since Erin's husband, Martin, died. Martin had been suffering from untreated depression. Erin had been concerned for his well-being, but Martin absolutely refused to seek professional help.

"On the day Martin disappeared, Erin left early for work, as she did every morning. When she arrived home that evening, Martin was gone, but that wasn't surprising. As hours passed she became more worried. She tried his cell—no answer. She finally went to bed. When she awoke the next morning, she saw he had not been home all night. She called his family and some close friends, but no one had seen him. Soon after, she found his cell phone, turned off, at home, along with his wallet, money, driver's license, and other documents. She reported his disappearance and an investigation began.

"A month later, Erin received a call from an officer saying that a body with no documents had been found hanging from a tree in a field. It was suspected to be and later identified as Martin's body. Erin and Kristin were devastated.

"Natasha doesn't fully realize how much support she has been to Erin, as well as being an advocate when Erin has felt engulfed in a situation not of her own making. Erin has needed someone to intercede for her, to be an ongoing advocate in the midst of bondage. The grace of Christ is present in Natasha and Erin's friendship. Erin opened the door to Natasha when she had no place to go due to a situation not of her own making. Now Natasha provides ongoing support and unconditional acceptance and care for Erin when she feels engulfed in her grief. Grace! Mutual ministry."

8. Weight of Sin/Weight Lifted

For many people sin is experienced not as guilt, or as being illegal, or even as being in some particular bondage, but more as a weight that can never be lifted. One is bowed down by burdens (its own kind of bondage), tired, unable to stand up straight, unable to reach out, even to God.

Our bodies can be weighed down, and so can our hearts. Sin is more than "bad actions." It is the burden of the complexity of human beings hurting one another. This results in being weighed down so that one cannot live freely. At times this weight is almost too great to bear individually and even communally.

The image that can free us is that this weight, whatever it is, no matter how longstanding or complex, has been lifted in the resurrection of Jesus. Millions of witnesses give us hope, and life, and freedom: "Since we are surrounded by so great a cloud of witnesses, let us also lay aside every weight and the sin that clings so closely . . ." (Heb 12:1). The word *weight* is used elsewhere in the Epistles, in a different way: "So we do not lose heart. . . . For this slight momentary affliction is preparing us for an eternal weight of glory beyond all measure" (2 Cor 4:16, 17). The weight is lifted and need never again hold us down.

The Airport Attendant

An airport attendant at Chicago O'Hare was pushing my wheelchair. She was behind me, of course, so I couldn't see her face as she adeptly made sure I made it from the gate to my connecting flight. But we engaged in conversation, so I began to see her as a person. She liked her job, she said. We talked some more. Then she moved beyond polite conversation and said that sometimes the weight was too heavy. She was small. When she needed to push a very large person with heavy bags, particularly up the jet bridge to the terminal, the weight was just too much for her. She added that sometimes another passenger exiting the plane would see how hard it was and would help her.

It's like that, isn't it? Sometimes we don't even see the face of someone who is bearing a weight that is too much for them to bear. The gospel message for them is not, "You are forgiven." Rather, because the ultimate weight of sin has been lifted in Christ, we are freed to put gospel into action and see the need, to help lift the weight for our neighbor, perhaps even the one serving us.

- What weight of sin lies heavy on your heart? Dwell on the reality that grace for you means that Christ has lifted that weight in the cross and resurrection. How does that change things even if the weight remains?

- How can we more clearly notice the weight that others bear? How can we together, in Christ, be of help in lifting those burdens?

CHAPTER 2

Darkness Turned to Light

The broad theme of darkness and light permeates this chapter as we explore eight images, two used often in the Epistles and six less frequently. We live in all kinds of darkness; Christ appears as the light in many ways. We live in the futility of being unenlightened about God; however, it is not enough to merely receive information *about* Jesus. Grace is the gift of wisdom . . . in the "foolishness" of the cross. Double-mindedness keeps our lives torn; grace through the mind of Christ provides singleness of purpose in vocation. Many people live under a dark cloud of feeling they are constantly being tested; Christ's own ultimate testing on the cross moves us into light. Being deceived leads people to believe darkly what is false. Our own human testimony needs the testimony of God in order to bring light to people's lives. The gospel shows that what was hidden is now revealed. Our own deluded identity is made clear so that in Christ we now reflect the image of God. Let us live into these images.

9. Darkness/Light

Rich Lives in the Light

Rich, who is visually impaired (legally blind), ministers in what people refer to as a forgotten neighborhood in Pittsburgh. Rich speaks about walking the neighborhood, sitting at the fire house, having coffee and connecting with people who are the working poor or unemployed. Even though he cannot see them, his insight enables him to describe them clearly. Serving ecumenically in diaconal community ministry, he moves throughout the neighborhood and within two congregations of different denominations. His wife, Pat, is pastor of one of those congregations.

Being able to use urban public transit has facilitated his ministry and outreach. Through his work on a neighborhood community council, Rich was invited to serve on the Ethics Committee of the city of Pittsburgh. He also serves on the Church and Society Committee and the Ecumenical Affairs Committee of his church body judicatory.

"For once you were in darkness" resonates with those whose lives, for any reason, are dark or seem dark. What kinds of darkness have been or are still part of your daily life? Illness? Depression? Despair? Blindness of any kind? "Darkness" also describes the human condition of not living in the light of God's grace in Jesus Christ. In Eph 5:8–9 Christians are challenged with the words, "For once you were darkness, but now in the Lord you are light. Live as children of light—for the fruit of the light is found in all that is good and right and true." This is not mere advice but declaration. Jesus Christ changes people so that they cease living in darkness and begin living in the light. Romans 13:12: "The night is far gone, the day is near. Let us then lay aside the works of darkness and put on the armor of light." The gospel *is* light. "For it is the God who said, 'Let light shine out of darkness,' who has shone in our hearts to give the light of the knowledge of the glory of God in the face of Jesus Christ" (2 Cor 4:6). And Christians share this light together.

Not only are Christians now *in* the light, but they *belong* to the light—they belong to the day: "But you, beloved, are not in darkness . . . for you are all children of light and children of the day; we are not of the night or of the darkness" (1 Thess 5:4–5). These verses refer to the Lord's coming; we should not "fall asleep," but since we "belong to the day" we should live in love and the hope of salvation through Jesus Christ (vv. 6–9).

In 1 Cor 4:5 the Lord's coming "will bring to light the things now hidden in darkness." First John 2 is clear that "whoever hates another believer is in the darkness, walks in the darkness, and does not know the way to go" (v. 11). And again, "The darkness is passing away and the true light is already shining. Whoever says, 'I am in the light,' while hating a brother or sister, is still in the darkness. Whoever loves a brother or sister lives in the light . . ." (vv. 8–10).

Jude 6 and 13 emphasize the power of "deepest darkness," that is, eternal darkness. God has "rescued us from the power of darkness" and transferred us into the kingdom of God's beloved Son (Col 1:13–14). The Epistle image of light brings hope.

People experience the depths of darkness and live in all kinds of darkness here on earth. For some the light of Christ may be a constant. For others it is a beacon in the distance, pointing the way. For some it is a small, flickering, but warm candle. Light may suddenly appear, or it may come slowly, almost imperceptibly, like the dawn.

Although these biblical references and our lives are in different contexts, there is consistency in that being in and belonging to the darkness is associated with old ways of living. Christ is the source of light, a "lamp shining in a dark place" (2 Pet 1:19). The work of Christ on the cross (when there was darkness at noon) transforms lives from darkness to light, now and in the kingdom for which Christians wait.

Rich will continue to live as a legally blind person, but his life, which has not been easy, has been transformed, he would say, again and again. When he entered seminary he was concerned about the unavailability of theological books for a person with impaired vision. Rich recalls, "The seminary president took my hand and said, 'We will do everything we can to make sure your needs are met,' and he did." (Pat met Rich when she became one of his readers.) Rich added, "Our seminary teaches students how to build community in their places of ministry."

Rich served for six years as a diaconal minister in prison chaplaincy in Michigan, which was an important ministry. While there he believed his inability to drive would not allow him to serve beyond institutional settings. Now, in partnership with Pat, but actually walking farther and farther out into the light of the neighborhood than she, he is building community all over the place. He says to the congregation he serves on Sundays, "We may be small, but the mission field around the church is full." When the church received some endowment money, he challenged them to fix the building, "So people can see you. We need to start acting like we are alive. We need to get ready for the people who are going to come." They also have begun an urban garden in a vacant lot next to the church.

Rich loves to paint—not "still life," but "what he sees in his head: geometric designs, illusions of movement, color and shape." This, ironically, is called "optical art." In the words of 1 John 1:5, "God is light," and in God there is no darkness at all.

- Where is there darkness in your life that others may not even notice? And where is there light in the midst of darkness?

- How does hearing that "Christ is light" and that "you belong to the light" have the potential for turning darkness into light in your daily life?

- In the midst of darkness, does light come as a small, flickering candle? Does it suddenly appear, or come slowly like the dawn?

10. Unenlightened/Wise

Jim: Seeking to Serve Wisely

Mark writes about accompanying Jim's seeking his sense of call: "Jim has been a school social worker for twenty-nine years, employed by an agency contracted by the state to serve public and private schools in a midsize city. He spends half his time working directly with teachers, parents, students, and school administrators and the other half filling out paperwork. The latter is increasing. Jim works hard, putting in ten-hour days and some weekend time. Even so, he laments, 'I am still behind on my forms.' Faculty and staff have been stunned and frustrated by the increase in documentation now mandated, particularly when each accrediting agency can decide what 'proficiency' means."

Mark notices that when Jim is not filling out forms, or tracking and filing forms, he spends a large amount of his time helping teachers do so, because they are under great pressure to avoid mistakes. So Jim not only provides instruction in filling out forms but also reassurance, encouragement, and a listening ear. This is his ministry, even when providing comfort and empathy may run counter to the mandate of his agency, which emphasizes results over relationships. So just what is knowledge? And how does one responsibly use information? And what does one's daily work have to do with human predicaments and the grace of God?

In 1 Corinthians 1 the cross is central and the image of unenlightenment, or "ignorance" and "foolishness," is prominently used alongside the image of grace as wisdom. The cross is "foolishness to those who are perishing," but power and wisdom to those who are being saved (v. 18). Christ crucified is a stumbling block to Jews and foolishness to Gentiles (v. 23). But "God's foolishness is wiser than human wisdom" (v. 25).

Paul writes that he decided to know nothing among the Corinthians except Jesus Christ crucified (1 Cor 2:2). He goes on to speak at length about God's wisdom—"not a wisdom of this age," but God's wisdom decreed before the ages (2:6–7). None of the rulers of the present age understood this, said Paul, or they would not have crucified Jesus (v. 8). No one could have conceived of what God had prepared (v. 9). First Corinthians 3:18–20 repeats the theme: "the wisdom of this world is foolishness with God," and God knows the futility of the thoughts of the wise. In receiving Christ, one becomes a fool in order to become wise. And once more in 1 Cor 4:10: "We are fools for the sake of Christ, but you are wise in Christ."

The human predicament is being without Christ, living "in the futility" of one's mind (Eph 4:17). People are "darkened in their understanding" because of their "ignorance" and "hardness of heart" (v. 18). In Romans we see the image of "senseless minds [being] darkened" and of people becoming "futile in their thinking" (1:21). People have a zeal for God, Paul says, "but it is not enlightened" (Rom 10:2). Being wise is a descriptor of being in Christ: living "not as unwise people but as wise . . ." (Eph 5:15). One no longer lives in foolishness but lives in wisdom; also, one is admonished not to *be* foolish but to "understand what the will of the Lord is" (v. 17).

This enlightened wisdom is part of the new covenant that is described in the Letter to the Hebrews. "I will put my laws in their minds, and write them on their hearts . . . and they shall not teach one another or say to each other, 'Know the Lord,' for they shall all know me . . ." (8:8–12; 10:16). So, how do we receive the enlightened wisdom of God?

It is the Spirit who reveals these things: "No one truly comprehends what is truly God's except the Spirit of God" (1 Cor 2:11). This is not the spirit of the world but God's Spirit, which enables us to receive, understand, teach, and interpret the gifts of the grace of God (1 Cor 2:10–14). Without the work of the Spirit, the gift is foolishness. Those who have received this gift are "subject to no one else's scrutiny" (v. 15). The passage culminates with the words, "We have the mind of Christ" (v. 16).

In 2 Cor 1:12 earthly wisdom is contrasted with the grace of God. Unenlightenment is not benign. In Titus 3:3 the writer describes his previous human predicament, admitting that "we ourselves were once foolish, disobedient, led astray, slaves to various passions and pleasures, passing our days in malice and envy, despicable, hating one another." And in 1 Tim 1:12–14, the writer confesses that he received mercy because he had acted ignorantly in unbelief in persecuting Christians. "The grace of our Lord overflowed for me with the faith and love that are in Christ Jesus" (v. 14). Likewise, enlightened understanding results in action. "Therefore prepare your minds for action" (1 Pet 1:13), and, "For it is God's will that by doing right you should silence the ignorance of the foolish" (1 Pet 2:15).

Mark discovered that Jim finds his greatest joy and sense of call when he helps teachers and parents deal with the most difficult situations, enabling them to overcome their confusion, fears, and frustrations even if it takes multiple sessions. Jim says, "Even professionals can get bogged down in terminology and facts and miss seeing the child. I love working with difficult children, even difficult parents. I see the biggest example of sin and its consequences not so much in bad behaviors and reactions, as in the way in which our educational system is forced to depersonalize the educational environment. Everyone becomes cases and statistics, and measurements of success need to be quantifiable and aggregate." This has led Jim many times to consider leaving this career behind. However, despite his having little hope that the systemic problems will change, he still cares deeply about families, children, and the schools.

Jim says that his Christian faith plays a vital role in his work and in his thought processes in "coping with this systemic sin and the brokenness of humanity" manifest in his workplace, in the people he serves, and in himself. A few years ago his own spiritual emptiness led him to understand that his thoughts were drenched in complaints, bitterness, and negativity. Through prayer, in worship and in community, he began a new way: to see God as wisdom and truth more present and active in his life and in others. This has made a difference in his sense of vocation.

In the Epistles, being saved means coming to the knowledge of the truth (1 Tim 2:4). It is not simply receiving information or knowing *about* Jesus. Knowledge means being enlightened by grace: "May grace and peace be yours in abundance in the knowledge of God and of Jesus our Lord" (2 Pet 1:2). One is saved from another *kind* of knowledge, which is the human predicament—for example, 1 Tim 6:20 reads, "Avoid the profane chatter and contradictions of what is falsely called knowledge." Likewise, in 1 Tim 1:6–7, where the writer warns against deviations from the faith, "meaningless talk." The writer of 1 Timothy is astonished that young Christians so quickly turn to a "different gospel," one that is contrary to the true gospel, the grace of Christ (Gal 1:6). The true gospel is "not of human origin" but a revelation of Jesus Christ, a gift from outside one's own knowing (v. 11). And this is not just personal knowledge, but communal: "I want their hearts to be encouraged and united in love, so that they may have all the riches of assured understanding and have the knowledge of God's mystery, that is, Christ himself" (Col 2:2–3).

The new life in Christ means being filled with "the knowledge of God's will in all spiritual wisdom and understanding" (Col 1:9). In Romans, being unenlightened is not understanding how to pray. God searches and knows the heart, and the Spirit intercedes "with sighs too deep for words" (Rom 8:26–27). And so we come to that often misused verse, "We know that all things work together for good for those who love God" (v. 28). Having explored the broad and deep uses of "knowing" that are rooted in the very saving act of Christ, we need to be careful to not quote just that one verse in a simplistic (and sometimes unhelpful) way. Who are we to "know" that someone else's tragedy will turn out for good for them?

Without the knowledge that *is* Christ, human beings seek to establish their own (Rom 10:3). This failure to understand hardens into claiming that one is wiser than one is (Rom 11:25). "O the depth of the riches and wisdom and knowledge of God!" (Rom 11:33–36). How unsearchable are God's judgments, and how inscrutable God's ways! We cannot know the mind of God, but having the wisdom that *is* Christ Jesus provides the gift of grace that makes all the difference in daily life.

- How is Jim seeking to serve wisely in the midst of constraining facts and figures? How does the image of grace as wisdom resonate with the issues you face in the arenas of your daily life?

- Having information and knowledge are hardly bad things. But what does it mean to still be unenlightened? How does God fill us with a different kind of wisdom in Christ?

- When does the gospel of Jesus Christ seem like mere "foolishness"? When have you felt as if you were left in the darkness of the futility of your own mind? How has God enlightened you through Scripture and through others?

11. Double-Minded/Single-Minded

Closely associated with but distinct from Unenlightened/Wise is this image. Sometimes we feel we are of two minds, divided in our sense of purpose, goal, even identity. We are torn, not really sure, not clear what to think or which way to go. The Epistle image of having the mind of Christ provides understanding, clarity, and unites us with others of the same mind. "We have the mind of Christ," Paul says in 1 Cor 2:16.

The term "double-mindedness" comes from Jas 4:8, where it is used to describe sinfulness. We are to "come to a sober and right mind" (1 Cor 15:34). The human predicament is also described as being "depraved in mind and bereft of the truth" (1 Tim 6:5), people of "corrupt mind and counterfeit faith" who "oppose the truth" (2 Tim 3:8). When have you felt like a counterfeit?

Likewise, Paul uses the term when describing how he comes across to those who see his witness: "if we are in our right mind, it is for you" (2 Cor 5:13). And this singled-mindedness, this being focused and determined, is centered in Christ, as Paul goes on, "For the love of Christ urges us on, because we are convinced that one has died for all: therefore all have died. And he died for all, so that those who live might live no longer for themselves, but for him who died and was raised for them" (2 Cor 5:14–15).

The Church Keeping Roy Focused

Listen to Bill's story of walking with Roy: "Roy owned and operated the town's bank, and, though now retired, he still serves on the board. He is known not only as one of the wealthiest but also as one of the most generous men in the area. He helped pay my way through school and helped make my house handicap accessible when my son was paralyzed. Roy readily agreed to have me walk with him through his day and asked me to meet him at his house for breakfast. He also asked me to wear something that I wouldn't mind getting dirty. When I arrived at Roy's house I found we were going to be spending the day helping area farmers with their wheat harvest by driving a grain truck and hauling wheat from the fields to the elevator.

"As we sat at the field watching the combines cutting the wheat, I asked how he had become involved in this. He told me that he has been helping out at harvest time since he was a young boy. 'There are a lot of people depending on the work these guys do and the crops they raise, from their own families to hungry people halfway around the world. As long as I'm able to get off my butt and give them a hand, I'll be out here doing whatever they need me to do.'

"I asked Roy if he ever thought of becoming a farmer instead of a banker and he said that God hadn't seen fit to give him the ability to be a successful farmer.

"I watched as people stopped to visit with Roy and was amazed at how he could give his full attention to each person while keeping an eye on the combines so he would be ready and in position the moment they needed him. Some people just stopped to talk; some spoke of family members who were ill; some told him about problems in their lives. Not once did I hear anyone ask Roy to step in and do something for them, and yet Roy didn't let a single person go by without taking some action to help. Sometimes he simply offered advice or empathy, but at other times his response was more substantial. At one point, when someone mentioned in passing that a single mother in town was having trouble finding a way to work because her car had broken down, I watched as Roy picked up his cell phone and coordinated with the local mechanic to have the car fixed and to send him the bill.

"When I asked Roy if he knew how blessed this community was to have him, he said, 'I'm not doing anything different than you, or these farmers, or anybody else in this town. We are all just working with the tools God gave us. All of us have something to offer. That's where the church comes in. The church keeps us focused, and we'll keep working.'"

Roy, the servant in the fields, has a clarity about the gospel and single-mindedness of purpose. Single-mindedness is most powerful in Phil 2:1–11, the "mind of Christ" passage:

> If then there is any encouragement in Christ, any consolation from love, any sharing in the Spirit, any compassion and sympathy, make my joy complete: be of the same mind, having the same love, being in full accord and of one mind. Do nothing from selfish ambition or conceit, but in humility regard others as better than yourselves. Let each of you look not to your own interest, but to the interests of others. Let the same mind be in you that was in Christ Jesus,
>> who, though he was in the form of God,
>>> did not regard equality with God
>>> as something to be exploited,
>> but emptied himself,
>>> taking the form of a slave,
>>> being born in human likeness.
>> And being found in human form,
>>> he humbled himself
>>> and became obedient to the point of death—
>>> even death on a cross.
>
> Therefore, God also highly exalted him

and gave him the name
that is above every name,
so that at the name of Jesus
every knee should bend,
in heaven and on earth and under the earth,
and every tongue should confess
that Jesus Christ is Lord,
to the glory of God the Father.

- When have you felt torn, not really sure what to think or which way to go? Who or what was pulling you in two or more directions?

- How is having the "mind of Christ" a gift of grace? Reflect on what that means for your sense of vocation, whether that be helping out at harvest, listening attentively, working for justice, or something else.

12. Tested/Entrusted

Cassandra's "Test"

"It was our very first conversation," said Cassandra. "We were beginning a new working relationship and were becoming acquainted. The man who would be my supervisor for this summer job asked questions. Things were going well. But then, after one of my responses, he said, 'Well, you passed that test.' I had not known I was being tested. After all, the contract had already been signed. Had he been grading each part of the conversation to see what I would say? Things would have begun so much differently had he trusted me as a coworker."

In our win-or-lose society, we often feel as though we are being measured all of the time. We suffer from a lack of trust. We often feel left in the dark, either from not knowing if and when we are being tested or from feeling we will never pass the tests those in power impose on us. We remain under a constant dark cloud.

Society, of course, conditions us to testing, to being tested: Dare I open this e-mail? Is someone trying to steal my data? Dare I "friend" this person or not? How can I verify a person's identity or credentials? We have been tested since birth. Growth charts. School grades. Job reviews. Many evaluations are important. Some testing promotes good health and growth. But many people feel they live under the constant threat of being tested and not passing, whatever "the test" may be. Such testing may be much deeper than a pop quiz or trick question. When have you been driven to the test—of strength, of faith, of suffering, of survival?

In the Letter to the Hebrews we see the "ancestors," the ancient Hebrew people, tested in their forty years in the wilderness (3:7–10). We also see Jesus, who had to become like the people in every respect, tested: "Because he himself was tested by what he suffered, he is able to help those who are being tested" (2:18).

Whatever the nature of the testing, we do not have a high priest (to use the language of Heb 4:15–16) who is unable to know or understand our situation, or sympathize with our weaknesses; rather, "we have one who in every respect has been tested as we are, yet without sin." Therefore, in the midst of the testing we can approach the "throne of grace with boldness so that we may receive mercy and find grace to help in time of need" (v. 16)

Christ was put to the ultimate test, and therefore, writes Paul in Rom 8:1–2, there is "now no condemnation for those who are in Christ Jesus." There is no testing for those who live in faith in Christ on this side of the cross and resurrection to see if they can be strong enough or good enough or smart enough to be loved by God. There is no more condemnation, and there need not be any lingering fear of not passing tests. In Jas 1:13–15 one reads, "No one, when tempted, should say, 'I am being tempted by God'; for God cannot be tempted by evil . . ." God tempts no one. God does not test or tempt for the fun of it, nor to prove God's own authority. God has all power and authority. Christ has already been tested. That was the ultimate test. The good news is trust.

We can be comforted even more when we hear that "no testing has overtaken you that is not common to everyone. God is faithful and will not let you be tested beyond your strength." With the testing God also will provide the way out so that we may be able to endure it (1 Cor 10:13). This is the new life in Christ. The testing of the heart is not a new trick or surprise exam. We have now been "approved by God to be entrusted with the message of the gospel . . ." (1 Thess 2:4).

The "test yourselves" of 2 Cor 13:5–7 is an invitation to see whether we are living in the faith. The words "unless you fail to meet the test" and "I hope you will find out that we have not failed" are words of concern from Paul and his companions about their own faithfulness in ministry. They want the Corinthians to be strong and true in their faith. The ultimate tests are over. The central question has been forever answered: "Do you not realize that Jesus Christ is in you?" With Christ in us, even unfair testing cannot cut us off from a trustworthy God. We no longer need to struggle in darkness, wondering who will test us or when we will be tested. The grace of God has been entrusted to us in Christ Jesus, who in turn entrusts us with ministry.

- What tests from the past do you remember? How might some still haunt you? Have you ever been unfairly tested? What does Christ having been ultimately tested mean to you?

- When have you felt you were facing a test that might be beyond your strength? What is your experience of finding it difficult to trust that God would enable you to endure the test? When have you trusted that God would help you find a way to endure?

- For what ministries are you entrusted?

13. Deception/Truth

Deceit is the way of the world, a practice as old as humankind itself. When have you been deceived? Has the life of your community been twisted by someone whose motives seemed to be true but were in the end false? In both letters to the Thessalonians, the writer acknowledges the human propensity to deceive and to be deceived. "The lawless one" (apparent in the working of Satan) is described as using every kind of wicked deception. Being engulfed in wicked deception includes living in the darkness of delusion, which leads people to believe what is false and therefore become unwilling and unable to love the truth (2 Thess 2:9–11). The writer to the Hebrews wants the brothers and sisters in the faith to exhort one another that none may be "hardened by the deceitfulness of sin" (Heb 3:13). In Jas 5:4 we see the picture of laborers who mowed the fields but the landowners kept back their wages by fraud and deception; their cries reached the ears of God.

"Let no one deceive you in any way" (2 Thess 2:3). False prophets "speak bombastic nonsense," we read, "and in their greed they will exploit you with deceptive words"; "the way of truth will be maligned" (2 Pet 2:18, 3, 2). But the appeal to believe the gospel "does not spring from deceit or impure motives of trickery" (1 Thess 2:3). The good news is that in the midst of a world of deceit, we have a God of truth.

The letters of John accentuate that no lie comes from the truth. The one who denies that Jesus is the Christ is the liar (1 John 2:21–22). John says, "I write these things to you concerning those who would deceive you" (v. 26). "The Son of God has come and has given us understanding so that we may know him who is true; and we are in him who is true, in his Son Jesus Christ. He is the true God and eternal life" (1 John 5:20). For John, abiding in Christ is abiding in the truth (1 John 2:27–28).

Deception will not cure itself. Its evil end is our living a lie and believing it to be the truth. When one learns the skill of deceiving, one will most likely continue to use it. And the particular predicament of deception is that we rarely know we are entangled in it at the time. We may think we are immune, but that in itself is self-deception. For example, we may hear people making promises of great financial gains ("if only you will . . .") that at first we easily dismiss, but soon we start to believe there may be some truth in these deceptions. And then we internalize the promises as truth. Deception may come from the inside as well as from those outside. Fill in the blanks of your own propensity toward self-deception. Once I begin to believe the lie, I will need to create another one to cover the first deception. The truth is buried.

Once we have been deceived, truth and trust seem impossible to reestablish. That is the human predicament. The radical good news of the gospel of Jesus Christ is that we no longer need to rely on deception. Deception does not and need not save us, our reputation, our sense of self, or our construction of reality. The gospel saves through the openness of the empty tomb shining a light on all of that deception. The God of truth is trustworthy and the Spirit can transform our motives, our attempts to hide, even our destructive skills and free us from the web of deception.

- When have you been deceived? How did you discover the deception?

- How does the truth of the gospel throw light on a deceptive situation, allowing you and all involved to turn from deceptive ways? What new trust will need to be established?

14. Human Testimony/Testimony of God

"Giving testimony" is familiar, even central, to some Christian denominations, while it is somewhat foreign to others. For these, giving "witness" might resonate more. Though differing in emphases and meaning, human beings' speaking about God has been an important practice throughout the ages and remains so today. We have a revealed God. It is amazing that God enlightens human beings through the words of other human beings, both in one-on-one conversation and in public places.

Our own human testimony needs the testimony of God in order to bring light to people's lives. "No prophecy ever came by human will, but men and women moved by the Holy Spirit spoke from God" (2 Pet 1:21). The three letters of John say much about human testimony. John was overjoyed to find people walking in the truth (2 John 4). In 3 John 3–4, addressing "the beloved Gaius," he writes, "I was overjoyed when some of the friends arrived and testified to your faithfulness to the truth, namely, how you walk in the truth. I have no greater joy than this, to hear that my children are walking in the truth." We are then not to be ashamed of the testimony about our Lord or of those who give it, including those who give it while in prison, but we are to join in their suffering, relying on the power of God (2 Tim 1:8). To have the courage to testify under difficult situations testifies to the grace of God.

But John also writes about people giving false testimony, putting themselves first, "spreading false charges," refusing to welcome friends and expelling them from the church (3 John 9–10). Likewise, in Jude 3–4 we see "certain intruders" who "pervert the grace of God" and "deny our only Master and Lord, Jesus Christ." There is human testimony and then there is human testimony! So it is throughout Scripture. Human testimony is both witness and barrier, promise and problem.

When we give testimony, whether through teaching, proclamation, personal instruction, witness, or casual conversation, what are we teaching? What are we proclaiming? To what or to whom are we bearing witness? How do we know our testimony is true and not simply self-aggrandizement, or unfounded gossip about someone we don't like? This is a predicament for both hearer and speaker.

The good news is that the Spirit is the one that testifies, for the Spirit is the truth (1 John 5:6–11). "There are three that testify: the Spirit and the water and the blood, and these three agree. If we receive human testimony, the testimony of God is greater" (vv. 7–9). The incarnation, death, and res-urrection of Christ is the testimony of God that God has testified to the son. "Those who believe in the Son of God have the testimony in their hearts" (v. 10). John goes on to say that those who do not believe in God have made God a liar by not believing in the testimony that God has given concerning the Son. John adds, "I write these things to you who believe in the name of the Son of God, so that you may know that you have eternal life" (v. 13).

We testify all the time. What are we talking about? We are so likely to be entangled in the thousands of words and testimonies we hear in our daily lives that we are left in the dark more than the light. The gospel is not just the mere words "Jesus Saves" on a bumper sticker. Grace is the living Word of Jesus Christ, revealed in the testimony of God, in which we are called to participate by our own transformed testimony.

- What do you talk about every day—at home, work, church? How does having Christ Jesus in your heart as the testimony of God change the very way you speak to people and listen to their words?

- Since one image of grace is being enlightened by God's testimony, how might you further prepare through education to teach and proclaim, converse and give enlightening witness or testimony, so that others might more surely know the grace of God in Christ Jesus?

15. Hidden/Revealed

Strange, perhaps, that even after the resurrection, salvation is hidden. Or perhaps it is not that Christ remains hidden, but that the human predicament keeps Christ hidden from us. Therefore our true, new selves, our gifts, our potential are likewise hidden from the world and even from ourselves. The writer to the Colossians says that he was commissioned to become a servant of the church, "to make the word of God fully known, the mystery that has been hidden throughout the ages and generations but has now been revealed . . ." (Col 1:25–26).

Salvation is hidden from us unless Jesus Christ is revealed to us. "Set all your hope on the grace that Jesus Christ will bring you when he is revealed" (1 Pet 1:13). Christ is revealed to us and faith is revealed to us (Gal 1:16; 3:23). "When Christ who is your life is revealed, then you also will be revealed with him in Glory" (Col 3:4). This salvation will be revealed even more fully in an unfading way in the last times, when Christ's glory is revealed (Rom 8:18 and 1 Pet 1:5, 7; 4:13; 5:1). We are not to live in judgment but to have a living hope in the grace of God through the resurrection of Christ, who "will bring to light the things now hidden in darkness" (1 Cor 4:5).

Just as that which is hidden is revealed, so Christ who is our light appears, when before we could not see the grace of God. For some of us the light of Christ was hidden our entire lives until God's grace was revealed.

Perhaps it still is hidden. For some of us, that light is hidden for a few days, or a few weeks, months, or even years. We express it in different ways; we might say, "I can't seem to see God's purpose in my life at all anymore," or "I can't see God in the world." We might sigh, "My day is all confusion. Everything is a blur," or ask, "The decision I have to make is hidden—where is God?" The good news is that God does not play hide-and-seek with us. God is here for us, now. We do not need to work to find God. God is looking to find us, as hidden as we may feel we are.

In Titus 2:11, we read, "For the grace of God has appeared, bringing salvation to all . . ." In 3:4–5 this is made even clearer: "When the goodness and loving kindness of God our Savior appeared, he saved us, not because of any works of righteousness that we had done, but according to his mercy, through the water of rebirth and renewal by the Holy Spirit." And then others can see Christ revealed through us.

Paul concludes the Epistle to the Romans by saying, "Now to God who is able to strengthen you according to my gospel and the proclamation of Jesus Christ, according to the revelation of the mystery that was kept secret for long ages but is now disclosed, and through the prophetic writings is made known to all the Gentiles, according to the command of the eternal God, to bring about the obedience of faith—to the only wise God, through Jesus Christ, to whom be the glory forever! Amen" (16:25–27).

- Have you ever felt that God, faith, or grace was just out of reach? That they were hidden someplace and could not be found? Do you still feel that way?

- The God who appeared, was incarnate, made flesh, as a baby, appeared to his disciples after death as the real, resurrected Christ. Where can you go to see that revealed God? How can you help others, who may feel as if God is hidden, also see this revealed God?

16. Deluded Identity/Image of God

We all delude ourselves from time to time. It's easier to delude ourselves if we are trying to hide from God or to hide from the truth. Or, when we begin to hide and then make a habit of it, we soon begin to delude ourselves and our image of ourselves. When we try so hard to be something or someone else, it becomes easier to imagine we are something or someone else. We fool ourselves. As we live more and more deeply into the reality that we have imagined for ourselves, the delusion grows. What was once light fades, then becomes darker and darker.

In Colossians, immediately following the phrase saying that God has rescued us "from the power of darkness" and transferred us into the kingdom of God's beloved Son, "in whom we have redemption, the forgiveness of sins," the Son is described as the "image of the invisible God" (Col 1:13–15). In Christ, the firstborn of all creation, all things in heaven and on earth were created, things visible and invisible, and all things were held together. This image of God as light itself is a complete image, for Christ is the "head of the body, the church; he is the beginning, the firstborn from the dead. . . . For in him all the fullness of God was pleased to dwell, and through him God was pleased to reconcile to Godself all things, whether on earth or in heaven, by making peace through the blood of his cross" (Col 1:16–20).

No one image connects to everyone; however, each image has the potential to reach someone at a particular time in that person's life. The human condition is complicated, involving internal relationships with self, all kinds of human relationships, and our relationship with God. That's why we have been calling it a "predicament." Sadly, deluded identities permeate our human relationships and transactions. Where is the light needed to see clearly? And, primarily, how can we see God? God, by grace, conveys God's own image upon us in Christ Jesus. And that changes everything!

- How has your sense of self changed through the years? Were there times when it has been unclear? How has this affected your relationships?

- What does it mean to you to live in the "image of God"? How is that good news?

The following story has elements of the above four images: Deception/Truth; Human Testimony/Testimony of God; Hidden/Revealed; and Deluded Identity/Image of God. Many of the stories in daily life are complex. We might find ourselves in many places in this story. We in the faith community find ourselves in differing positions. All, including those who lived before and those who will live after us, are entangled in the human predicament.

John: Feeling Deceived and Conflicted

Listen as Dan walks with John: "Things have changed recently for John, who is angry with the prospects of strip-mining, nearly a *fait accompli* in his region. He and his family are firmly rooted in the ground from which they derive their existence, rooted in God's creation. John feels deceived by the intentions of those with no ties to the land coming to the area and promising monumental change. 'Big Oil,' as it has been named locally, has identified this area as an epicenter of 'frack' sand and as desired for 'fracking' the earth's crust to mine the oil and natural gas hidden beneath. John sees the despoilment of the natural beauty and is aghast that many of his neighbors are willing to cooperate with Big Oil, receiving inordinately high prices for land leases. Are they being deceived?

"John leads an adult Bible study at his home church. Right now they are studying Genesis and the human condition, the simultaneous "saint and sinner" nature of people. He and the group are struck by the faithfulness of Abraham in the face of external factors. Oil companies obtain land leases through their company representatives, who offer large amounts of money that are nearly impossible to turn down. One small farmer, whose farm happened to be well situated, sold his land for forty million dollars over the course of several years. John believes that there is probably nothing illegal about representatives of Big Oil—regular people, saints and sinners—advocating for their company, but that there is certainly, from his viewpoint, something that deludes, hides the dangers, if not actually deceives.

"John wonders about the moral implications of the Big Oil representatives co-opting landowners to engage in an activity that may prove, in the long run, to be directly opposed to their several interests. John, even though he is so passionate about this issue, believes that is why all of us need God in our lives—to put a framework around the exercise of our various vocations. John is conflicted with the sense of what is considered deception and what is considered truth. In several public meetings the populace has been assured that the environmental impact of fracking is negligible. Yet John balances this against Big Oil's reluctance to publicly provide impact studies that contain quantifiable measurements of pollutants and other adverse byproducts generated by established mines.

"John is horrified when he considers how strip mines will affect this beautiful area of creation. Property values, now high, may plummet. The presence of open-pit mining will blight this pristine area. What is the real cost of 'progress'? This issue has pitted neighbor against neighbor. Advocacy groups for both sides have formed, and they have frequently been publicly at odds. Some understand the positions taken by both sides, but most are on one side or the other. Tension exists in the community, with some hoping for the huge payday."

- How does the church, or each particular church community, address environmental issues?

- What is deception in this story, even when people may have their own good intentions? How are insights, information, and viewpoints hidden? In our own lives, how can our true identity on an issue become deluded? Grounded in our own values, how can our own testimony escalate into divisions?

- What is the good news of God's grace in such a situation? How does living in the truth of God's revelation help faith communities assess motivations and discern vocation? How does living in the image of God help a community maintain a sustainable environment and care for the neighbor, near and far?

CHAPTER 3

From Death into Life

This chapter includes nine images. The Death/Life image itself is a major one in the Epistles (both death of the body and being dead in sin). Our hope is in the resurrection of Jesus Christ. Therefore, we are reconciled and no longer enemies of God or of one another. Destruction is a deathlike experience, whether experienced suddenly or daily; we are called to be part of God's gracious action of rescue. Closely associated is the image of a shaking world where Christ alone provides a firm foundation. Christ was crucified in weakness so that we might be strong by the power of the Spirit. The minor images of Old Yeast/Unleavened Bread and Decay/Fruit show us the whole creation and the life-giving nature of fruit-bearing lives. Similarly, the image of Waterless Places/Life-giving Waters makes us ponder the human predicament being like a waterless place. The chapter concludes with the image of Christ abolishing death forever.

17. Death/Life

Moving from death into life is a central image of grace in Christ. This new life is plural. Christians are made alive *together*. This image relates to actual death of the body, such as in 1 Thess 4:13–14. We are not to grieve as others who have no hope, "for since we believe that Jesus died and rose again, even so, through Jesus, God will bring with him those who have died." And "whether we are awake or asleep we may live with him" (5:10).

The image also relates to being dead in sin: "You were dead through trespasses and sins in which you once lived" (Eph 2:1). God, who is rich in mercy, out of the great love with which God loved us "even when we were dead through our trespasses, made us alive together with Christ—by grace you have been saved" (Eph 2:4–5).

The death and resurrection of Christ has consequences for life now, as we see in 2 Cor 5:15: "And he died for all, so that those who live might live no longer for themselves, but for him who died and was raised for them." Once again the reference is plural and the new life is for the sake of other people and Christ himself.

All three—death and life of the body, death to sin and life as salvation, and new life as service to other people—are part of Jan's story, as told by Josh.

Jan's Source of Life

Josh writes about visiting Jan's world of vocation: "Every time I see her she looks the same. Her face carries expressions of happiness and exhaustion. Today is no different. Her disheveled black hair shows signs that she has long been at work, even though it is only eight in the morning. She approaches me with a smile. Jan is a proud and dedicated hard worker at the food bank. 'It's a good job,' she says. 'Long hours? Sure! But I love what I do.'

"As I began to place items on my cart, Jan looked across the room toward another patron, saying, 'I'll catch you in a minute.' I noticed how she effortlessly approaches patrons and initiates conversation, making people feel welcome, as if they are entering the café or grocery store.

"Later that morning Jan was approached by a patron who was angry that all of the red meat had been taken earlier. This was not an uncommon remark from him. She later said to me, 'It takes all kinds, doesn't it?' 'How do you do it?' I asked. 'How do you deal with angry people?' She smiled back, took a deep breath, looked at the floor and sighed. I asked her to join me for a cup of coffee. She nodded silently and we went from the warehouse to the office. As we sat down, tears began to flow. She said, 'Sometimes this is a hard place to work. We try so hard to find the right things for people. I wish we had more. I wish we would never run out.'

"Jan went on to say that she had recently lost her husband unexpectedly. She was worried about what would happen to their home and how she would survive on one income. She said her children were providing support, but she didn't want to be a burden to anyone.

"I asked her, 'How are you taking care of yourself?' I'll never forget her response. She looked up; glancing toward the pictures around the room of smiling patrons and overstocked warehouse shelves, she smiled and sighed, 'This place takes care of me. This is Gospel.'

"Jan's work at the food bank, though hard and emotionally draining at times, brings with it healing and nourishing energy to deal with the daily struggles in her own life. And it doesn't end at the food bank. Jan also volunteers on a number of boards and nonprofit agencies. Jan, to her very core, is a source of life.

"Jan sees those who enter the food bank as equally children of God. Most of the patrons are shopping for agencies around the area rather than for themselves. Shopping in a food bank is a humbling experience. I remember how I felt the first time. Jan, however, is able to show grace to even the most demanding or despondent patron, seeing people in the image of God no matter how they feel about themselves or how others may think about them."

Death and Life as a Comprehensive Image

In Philippians Paul struggles and boldly says, "For to me, living is Christ and dying is gain" (Phil 1:21). Even more powerful is Phil 3:10: "I want to know Christ and the power of his resurrection . . ." Christ *emptied* himself and *humbled* himself, becoming "obedient to the point of death—even death on a cross" (Phil 2:8), then was exalted by God (v. 9). The image of death and life is a comprehensive image.

We "take hold of the life that really is life" (1 Tim 6:19). Jesus Christ "abolished death and brought life and immortality to light through the gospel" (2 Tim 1:10). "Jesus Christ raised from the dead" is "my gospel" (2 Tim 2:8). Then that central passage: "The saying is sure: If we have died with him, we will also live with him . . ." (2:11). And in the First Letter of John: "this life was revealed, and we have seen it and testify to it, and declare to you the eternal life that was with the Father and was revealed to us" (1 John 1:2). And, "Whoever has the Son has life; whoever does not have the Son of God does not have life" (1 John 5:12).

In 1 Peter, this new life is like a "new birth" and "a living hope through the resurrection of Jesus Christ from the dead" (1:3); it is like being "born anew, not of perishable but of imperishable seed, through the living and enduring word of God" (1:23).

In 1 Cor 15:12ff. we find the long discourse on the question of the resurrection. "If Christ has not been raised, then our proclamation has been in vain and your faith has been in vain" (v. 14). Without Christ having been raised, "you are still in your sins" (v. 17). Although this refers to the resurrection of the dead, Paul also says that he "dies every day" (v. 31), broadening the Death/Life image to include the deathly experiences in this life. To have new life in Christ now is to live with a new kind of hope beyond merely human hopes (v. 32).

Romans 4:25 says that Jesus was "handed over to death for our trespasses and was raised for our justification." "For the wages of sin is death" (Rom 6:23). "Who will rescue me from this body of death?" (Rom 7:24). God "gave life to the dead" (Rom 4:17). And in Rom 5:12–17 is the longer discourse on how death came through sin and exercised dominion: "If the many died through the one man's trespass [Adam's sin], much more surely have the grace of God and the free gift in the grace of the one man, Jesus Christ, abounded for the many" (v. 15). Death exercised dominion, but now the free gift of righteousness exercises dominion in life through Jesus Christ (v. 17). Romans 7:7–13 is the long discourse on how apart from the law sin lies dead. When sin revived, "I died" (v. 10). "Sin, seizing an opportunity in the commandment, deceived me and through it killed me" (v. 11).

This image appears, frequently, in regard to being dead in trespasses (Col 2:13). We are being made alive *together* with him. Christians were "buried with Christ in baptism" and "raised with him through faith in the power of God, who raised him from the dead" (Col 2:12).

Now that we are alive, "Should we continue in sin in order that grace may abound? By no means! How can we who died to sin go on living in it?" (Rom 6:2). And, "Do you not know that all of us who have been baptized in Christ Jesus were baptized into his death? Therefore we have been buried with him by baptism into death, so that, just as Christ was raised from the dead by the glory of the Father, so we too might walk in newness of life. For, if we have been united with him in a death like his, we will certainly be united with him in a resurrection like his" (Rom 6:3–5). This continues in verses 8–11: "If we have died with Christ, we believe that we will also live with him. We know that Christ, being raised from the dead, will never die again; death no longer has dominion over him. The death he died, he died to sin, once for all; but the life he lives, he lives to God. So you also must consider yourselves dead to sin and alive to God in Christ Jesus." Having been joined together in Christ's death and new life, nothing can separate us from God or from each other in Christ. "For I am convinced that neither death, nor life . . . will be able to separate us from the love of God in Christ Jesus our Lord" (Rom 8:38–39).

Paul says that since he has been crucified with Christ, "it is no longer I who live, but it is Christ who lives in me. And the life I now live in the flesh I live by faith in the Son of God, who loved me and gave himself for me" (Gal 2:19–20). Christ now lives in and through us.

Christians, as they live and as they die, are united with Christ in service to others: "We do not live to ourselves, and we do not die to ourselves. If we live, we live to the Lord, and if we die, we die to the Lord; so then, whether we live or whether we die, we are the Lord's. For to this end Christ died and lived again, so that he might be Lord of both the dead and the living" (Rom 14:7–9).

The image of death and life is central and permeates the Epistles. Surely it is core to being joined with Christ in a resurrection like his. It also pertains to the deathlike experiences of daily struggle. Paul writes of his afflictions, "for we were so utterly, unbearably crushed that we despaired of life itself. Indeed, we felt that we had received the sentence of death so that we would rely not on ourselves but on God who raises the dead" (2 Cor 1:8–9). And in Philippians, "I want to know Christ and the power of his resurrection and the sharing of his sufferings by becoming like him in his death, if somehow I may attain the resurrection from the dead" (3:10–11). The good news is that the daily deaths of suffering and bereavement, as well as death itself, no longer have the final word. "If we have died with him, we will also live with him." The compilation of Scripture passages from the Epistles, from so many different contexts, is so rich—and there are many more than are mentioned here. Suffice it to say that the image of grace as life over death is one of the central images in the Epistles.

- What have been your experiences with death? How, in Christ, does it no longer hold dominion over you? What are some of your daily "little deaths"? How does Christ bring new life in those situations?

- What does it feel like to be "dead in sin"? What would it mean for a community to be dead in systemic sin? How does the death and resurrection of Christ put sin to death, that we might be raised with Christ?

- How can Jan's life be Gospel? What images of grace do you see in people's vocation bringing new life to those living in deathly situations, whether physically, psychologically, or otherwise?

18. Enemies/Reconciled

Can you imagine what it would be like to be an enemy of God? God who is the almighty creator and ruler of the universe? As unfathomable as God's own self is, the concept of being God's enemy is greater; and yet, many people often feel that God is their enemy and that they are an enemy of God. In Rom 5:6–10, Paul uses progressively strong words: while we were "weak," "ungodly" (think for a minute what that word might really mean) "sinners" and finally subject to God's "wrath," we were named "enemies."

A heavy word, and yet we are enemies of God's will when we corrupt the creation, kill human beings whom God also loves, and create enmity within our families. The list is long. It is a deathly list. We so often persist in dwelling there as though there is no other way to be, to live with one another, and to live in the presence of God. However, the key passage of this image makes all the difference in our lives: "For if while we were enemies, we were reconciled to God through the death of God's Son, much more surely, having been reconciled, will we be saved by his life" (Rom 5:10). While! Not *after* we stopped our behavior. Not *after* we stopped being enemies of God or of one another, but *while.* The emphasis on God's action is underscored in a previous sentence: ". . . while we still were sinners Christ died for us" (v. 8). Paul goes on, "But more than that, we even boast in God through our Lord Jesus Christ, through whom we have now received reconciliation" (v. 11).

If God is not our enemy, then there is no condemnation: "There is therefore now no condemnation for those who are in Christ Jesus" (Rom 8:1). And the condemnation of others, however harsh, cannot trump God: "If God is for us, who is against us?" (8:31). We now have the opportunity to live without fear of what enemies can ultimately do to us, except of course death itself.

In 1 Cor 15:24–28 there is a section on Christ's death and resurrection and the end time that describes how every ruler and authority and power must finally be subjected. Here is named the final "enemy," death itself (v. 26). Death is the enemy. We do people no favors when we try to soften death by saying it is God's will that babies die, that thousands starve, or that God wants certain nations to be decimated in war. Death is the enemy. Christ died and death no longer has the final word. The gospel word is reconciliation. The gospel action is the ministry of reconciliation.

Grace in this image is the gift that in Christ we are no longer enemies of God or of one another, but are reconciled to God and also to one another. Whether the conflict is that of warring nations, or competitors in the workplace, or feuding family members, we have the promise of reconciliation as a gift. And, beyond that we have been given the gift of the ministry of reconciliation. "All this is from God." God reconciled us to Godself through Christ "and has given us the ministry of reconciliation." God was and is at work in Christ, reconciling the world to God's own self and "entrusting the message of reconciliation to us" (2 Cor 5:18–19).

This is an amazing gift, work, responsibility, and calling. The very ones who were enemies are now the reconciled ones. That means we may live new lives—no longer mired in denial, pretending that everything is okay in our relationships, but trusting that we are already reconciled to God and to one another. So, "we are ambassadors for Christ." We are told, "Be reconciled to God" (2 Cor 5:20–21). This is both descriptive and imperative; it is a new living reality. Trusting this reconciling God, we are called to live out this reconciliation in the closest of relationships—which are sometimes the hardest—and in difficult, complex global entanglements. We are called to be ministers of reconciliation, empowered by a God of reconciliation.

- When in your life have you felt the deathly experience of being someone's enemy? Of feeling you were an enemy of God?

- Ponder Christ's work of taking on the worst enemy—death itself. How does that impact the way you view death? Life? How do you talk about death and life?

- What ministry of reconciliation might Christ be calling you to right now? What other ministries of reconciliation might you be called to? What ministries might your faith community, your city, and even your nation be called to in the world?

19. Destruction/Rescue

Destruction and Rescue in a Chilean Mine

The Copiapó mining accident began on the afternoon of Thursday, August 5, 2010, as a significant cave-in deep in Chile's Atacama Desert, one of the driest and harshest regions on earth. In the aftermath of the destruction, the thirty-three miners survived for sixty-nine days nearly half a mile underground, though it was originally thought that they probably had not survived the collapse or would starve to death before they were found—if they were ever found. During a period of great uncertainty, seventeen days after the accident, on August 22, a note written in bold red letters appeared taped to a drill bit when it was pulled to the surface. It read simply, "Estamos bien en el refugi" (We are well in the shelter). The image of grace as destruction and rescue was used over and over to describe the enormous grief and fear and the huge relief and celebration. The nation of Chile, and the world, erupted into a wave of euphoria.

The Human Communal Problem of Destruction

How does one explain the great loss of life in a tornado, hurricane, or earthquake? How does one deal with such destruction? How does one explain, particularly to oneself, one's survival when a neighbor's house has been destroyed? Just what kind of a God do we have, anyway? In Eph 2:3 we read, "We were by nature children of wrath, like everyone else." Destruction, wrath, even being under a "curse" are all part of the human predicament. So often we want to rationalize that the "bad ones" (people, nations, or races) deserved wrath and destruction, while the "good ones," who kept God's laws, deserved rescue. But the Epistles make it clear that all who rely on the works of the law "are under a curse" (Gal 3:10). Further, "Christ redeemed us from the curse of the law by becoming a curse for us . . ." (Gal 3:13).

The law brings wrath, but where there is no law, neither is there violation (Rom 4:15). And then come these words of relief: "Much more surely then, now that we have been justified by his [Jesus] blood, will we be saved through him from the wrath of God" (Rom 5:9). This wrath is real; it is past—it was dealt with on the cross—and yet it still exits through the power of Satan's evil. "The God of peace will shortly crush Satan under your feet. The grace of our Lord Jesus Christ be with you" (Rom 16:20). In the midst of all the destruction we have seen or can imagine, Christ wipes away destruction. Through death Christ destroys "the one who has the power of death, that is, the devil" (Heb 2:14).

"Destruction" is also used as an image of the end time. It will come like a thief in the night (1 Thess 5:1–11). "When they say, 'There is peace and security,' then sudden destruction will come upon them, as labor pains come upon a pregnant woman, and there will be no escape!" (vv. 2–3). But for the children of day "God has destined us not for wrath but for obtaining salvation through our Lord Jesus Christ" (v. 9). People have real questions—and fear—concerning this. How much more important to focus on the Christ who has rescued all in the cross and now calls us to ministries of care and rebuilding when people face earthly destruction.

The "lawless" one is destined for destruction (2 Thess 2:1–12). It is this one who exalts himself. Satan deceives and so people perish because they refuse to love the truth and be saved (vv. 9–10). In contrast, "The Lord is faithful" and "will strengthen you and guard you from the evil one" (2 Thess 3:3). In 2 Tim 4:17–18, we find the same image of being strengthened by God: "But the Lord stood by me and gave me strength, so that through me the message might be fully proclaimed and all the Gentiles might hear it. So I was rescued from the lion's mouth. The Lord will rescue me from every evil attack . . ."

We often imagine rescue in miraculous, even grandiose ways, such as the global story of the miners in Chile. However, the image of rescue is also used in the Epistles to describe God's action in Christians' daily lives. God rescues daily for purposeful ministry. We are called to be part of God's grace in actions of ongoing rescue. Paul says that the God "who rescued us from so deadly a peril will continue to rescue us"; on this God's people have set their hope that God will rescue them again (2 Cor 1:10).

"Rescue" is used almost simultaneously with the trials of daily life because it *is* for daily life, not just for the end time. In 2 Thess 3:1–3 we read, "Pray for us . . . that we may be rescued from wicked and evil people; for not all have faith. But the Lord is faithful . . ." Scripture also uses rescue in regard to the end time in saying that God raised Jesus from the dead: "Jesus, who rescues us from the wrath that is coming" (1 Thess 1:10).

Destruction is more than surprising. It is the reality in which humankind lives. It is communal even when some are seemingly rescued and others die. God is not intent on punishing one and not another; all live in this human and global reality of destruction. God destroys the destroyer through Christ and rescues us from ultimate destruction, calling us to lives not of fear and speculation but of courage and care. Sometimes that takes amazing communal strength. Sometimes it takes just one person with a caring heart.

- When have you been overwhelmed, or almost overwhelmed, by destruction? How did you interpret its coming, its power, its source? Wrath, luck, fate? Good people and bad people?

- How do you see Christ's death and resurrection as God's rescue of humankind now and ultimately?

- How have you been called to participate in the ministry of rescue in daily life?

20. A Shaking World/A Firm Foundation

"God is a God not of disorder but of peace" (1 Cor 14:33). Whether in terms of relationships, ecclesial matters, or physical realities, the world we experience is often marked by disorder. Our world shakes inside and outside. This, however, is not the nature of God. The God of calm not chaos, the Christ of Peace, provides a firm foundation when the world is shaking. Not that God is bereft of power, as the writer of Hebrews makes clear, writing of the time when God's voice "shook the earth." The writer goes on, "Yet once more I will shake not only the earth but also the heaven" (12:26). The writer interprets this to mean that "yet once more" indicates the removal of created things so that "what cannot be shaken may remain. Therefore since we are receiving a kingdom that cannot be shaken, let us give thanks, by which we offer to God an acceptable worship with reverence and awe" (vv. 27–28).

We have a God who can shake the world in an instant, whose power is greater than all that would shake us, and who has given us in Christ a new realm, a place that cannot be shaken or taken from us. Therefore Paul says in 2 Cor 1:7 that "our hope for you is unshaken." Particularly in times of anxiety, not only do we have a "little" hope, but great hope through Christ who provides a firm, unshakable foundation for life to continue.

Like the early church, faith communities today can easily be shaken, filled with anxiety. The word to the brothers and sisters is "not to be quickly shaken in mind or alarmed" (2 Thess 2:2), not because there are not good reasons (then or today), such as conflict and deception, but because this image of grace reminds us that the foundation, when all is shaken, remains firm. Likewise, in 2 Tim 2:19, we have the same image: "God's firm foundation stands." Therefore, we are called upon to live "in a manner worthy of the gospel of Christ . . . standing firm in one spirit, striving side by side with one mind for the faith of the gospel" (Phil 1:27).

The 2010 Haiti Earthquake

As those first terrible hours unfolded we all tried every possible social media connection to find out what had happened to our four Wartburg Seminary students serving and studying during J-Term 2010. Three were in Port-au-Prince. The earthquake in Haiti was devastating, and we knew even then that the death toll would be unimaginable.

Finally we heard: Renee Splichal Larson had survived, but her husband, Ben, had not. Renee, Ben, and Ben's cousin, Jonathan Larson, had returned to St. Joseph's Guest House after a day of working in Port-au-Prince. As Renee later told us, they were sitting at a table in a large room when things started to shake. They all started to run. Renee saw Jon out of the corner of her eye and began to wonder where Ben was. She turned and saw him steadying himself by a pillar in the middle of the room. And then suddenly the two floors and roof of concrete above caved in on them. After the crash, Jon and Renee realized they were alive but thought they would die from suffocation in the debris. Slowly they made their way out—but, Renee said, "All I could think about was Ben. I felt so helpless and powerless." Jon and Renee were now virtually on the top of what remained of the building. "Looking out over the city, all we could see was a cloud rising up as we heard the cries of the people," she said.

Renee went on: "People said, 'Don't go back in,' but at that moment I didn't care if I died; I just wanted to find Ben." She did go back in; at least she could make her way far enough back in to hear Ben's voice. "He was singing," Renee said. "It was to the tune of the hymn 'Where Love and Charity Abide.' I remember his last two lines: 'O Lamb of God, you bear the sin of all the world away; eternal peace with God you made, God's peace to us we pray.' And then it was silent. Jon and I told him we were OK. I told him that I loved him."

Even though they didn't want to leave, they had to. They spent that night outside in an open field with thousands of others. The aftershocks continued. The shaking of the foundations. The shaking of people's lives.

The earth shook at the moment of Christ's death. Christ's death and resurrection are more powerful than our powerlessness. In the midst of a shaking world, we are already in a place that cannot be shaken, as counter as that seems to all of our senses. There will be the removal of what is shaken, so that what cannot be shaken may remain. We are receiving a kingdom that cannot be shaken.

Renee is now pastor of Heart River Lutheran Church in Mandan, North Dakota. The vocation of that congregation has been to worship every Sunday morning for thirty years with incarcerated youth on the campus of the North Dakota Youth Correctional Center. She and Jon are now married and have a child. Preaching at the ELCA churchwide assembly on August 25, 2011, Renee included in her powerful sermon these words: "Do justice. Water crisis, world hunger, AIDS, racism, genocide, war, sexism, corruption, malaria, self-service, and natural disasters are just a few of the overwhelming injustices happening in the world. Fellow children of God, where do we even begin?

"Weeping people are not so incapacitated that they cannot live out their baptismal calling to witness to the hope they have in Jesus Christ. Justice cries out for the resurrection from the sorrow-filled, exhausted heart. The earthquake did not care who was wealthy or poor, laughing or weeping, hungry or full. A common phrase on the streets of Haiti is: 'Everyone lost someone; someone lost everyone.' In fact I met a Haitian man this morning who is a worker in a hotel who lost twenty-five family members in less than a minute. Can we imagine the sorrow?

"I am a witness to sorrow, death, and for me, the world coming to an end; yet, I am also a witness to hope in the power of God to make all things new. I am a witness to the Haitian people gathering together the night of the earthquake and for weeks after in song and prayer. We are marked with the cross of Christ forever, and sealed by the Holy Spirit who leads and empowers us in the way of justice and peace. You are ready to be moved and disrupted by the Spirit and the abundant and amazing grace of God."

- When have you felt as if your very foundations were being shaken, or a "roof" caving in over your head?

- Since Christ has provided an unshakable new place to be in God's presence, how has the Spirit, in the midst of your weeping, provided hope for life-giving works of justice?

21. Weakness/Strength

Dorothee Soelle wrote in her book *The Strength of the Weak* that Christ did not want to be strong except through the solidarity of the weak.[1] In 2 Cor 13:3–4 we read, "He is not weak in dealing with you, but is powerful in you. For he was crucified in weakness, but lives by the power of God. For we are weak in him, but in dealing with you we will live with him by the power of God." In addition, we have verse 9, "for we rejoice when we are weak and you are strong. . ." In Rom 5:6 we read, "for while we were still weak, at the right time Christ died for the ungodly." The writer of Hebrews also uses the image in saying that "we do not have a high priest who is unable to sympathize with our weaknesses . . ." (4:15).

There are numerous verses speaking of God's power in the saving action of Christ. Romans 1:4 shows the Son of God declared with power according to the spirit of holiness by the resurrection from the dead. The gospel is the "power of God for salvation to everyone who has faith, to the Jew first and also to the Greek" (Rom 1:16). And weakness may be described as woundedness. By Christ's "wounds you have been healed" (1 Pet 2:24). However, God's power in the saving action of Christ may or may not produce healing and strength for individuals or communities.

Christians continue to deal with being weak—for example, "the Spirit helps us in our weakness; for we do not know how to pray as we ought, but that the very Spirit intercedes with sighs too deep for words" (Rom 8:26). In Rom 14:1 we read that we are to "welcome those who are weak in faith, but not for the purpose of quarreling over opinions." In the faith community the strong ought to "put up with the failings of the weak" (Rom 15:1).

Christ understands weakness and was crucified in weakness so that we might be strong by the power of the Spirit. But such strength is not for our own boasting or to be used in order to "conquer for Christ." The strong are strong so that they might welcome the weak. Weakness is made strong in Christ Jesus. In fact, weakness is transformed. It is no longer weakness. We do not know Paul's "weakness," and perhaps it is just as well, because many of us can then relate in our own diverse weaknesses. "What is uncontested is that amid his afflictions and weaknesses, Paul boasted in the power of Christ. . . . We should not underestimate the significant role that physical

1. Dorothy Soelle, *The Strength of the Weak,* trans. Robert Kimber and Rita Kimber (Philadelphia: Westminster, 1984) 30.

infirmity played in shaping Paul as the first theologian of weakness."[2] As he says in 2 Cor 12:5, "I will not boast, except of my weaknesses." And he testifies that God said to him after he appealed to God three times, "'My grace is sufficient for you, for power is made perfect in weakness.' So I will boast all the more gladly of my weaknesses, so that the power of Christ may dwell in me. Therefore I am content with weaknesses . . . for the sake of Christ: for whenever I am weak, then I am strong" (2 Cor 12:5, 8–10).

My Story of Weakness Transformed

Into this image I will insert part of my own story—living for more than thirty years with the weakness of a chronic illness. I have a disease; I am not my disease. Supported and respected by a caring seminary community I have been able to teach, write, and lecture here and around the world, but not without limitations.

When people encounter someone with a disability and are made aware of their own vulnerability, they may become fearful. Fear for themselves, fears for me and about me. People in this "move-on" culture want me to be "over" my disease and my weakness: "You're looking good. You're feeling better now, aren't you?" Instead of saying, "I'll never be totally better," I respond, "I'm feeling well enough, thank you." I am well enough to listen carefully to students. I am professor, counselor, and mentor. I am well enough to teach and preach with vitality and passion. I especially enjoy creating an environment in which everyone's voice comes alive. Then, after class, I rest. I rest. I rest.

I'm tired of resting. Many mornings I need courage to start the day. A sense of vocation and faith in a God of grace give me power to be a servant in a world in need. I sit to teach, to preach, and to administer the sacraments. Initially concerned that my disability would be a distraction, I have found it provides a connection. As people come forth to receive bread and wine, our eyes meet and we are all strengthened.

Many people living with myalgic encephalomyelitis become homebound, isolated from the world. I am blessed with a husband who has lovingly stood by me, who asks and who seeks to understand, and also with compassionate grown sons and their families. I think, "Some people have

2. Amos Yong, *The Bible, Disability, and the Church* (Grand Rapids: Eerdmans, 2011) 89.

it much worse; my problems are nothing in comparison." But weakness is not a competitive sport.

Weakness is transformed and so is power as we see in 2 Corinthians: "For he was crucified in weakness, but lives by the power of God. For we are weak in him, but in dealing with you we will live with him by the power of God" (13:4).

We pray for each other in weakness and pray for each other to have power: I pray that "you may be strengthened in your inner being with power . . ." (Eph 3:16); "Finally, be strong in the Lord," which is followed by the "whole armor of God" passage (Eph 6:10–17); "May you be made strong with all the strength that comes from his glorious power . . ." (Col 1:11).

The image of power as grace is not power over another: "We rejoice when we are weak and you are strong" (2 Cor 13:9). The new life in Christ means that when you have more power I do not have less, and when I have more power you do not have less, because the Spirit's power is unlimited. We are no longer afraid to be weak in the presence of the other and need no longer be afraid of the other's power. Transformation. Grace!

- What is your weakness? Does it make you embarrassed? Dependent? Discouraged?

- How has God given you power through weakness? How might God empower you?

22. Old Yeast/Unleavened Bread

Each of the images of grace included in this collection is directly connected to the work of Christ. So it is with this image, too, which is mentioned only briefly. In 1 Cor 5:6–8, a warning against boasting, we read, "For our paschal lamb, Christ, has been sacrificed. Therefore, let us celebrate the festival, not with the old yeast, the yeast of malice and evil, but with the new unleavened bread of sincerity and truth." The old batch is cleaned out so that we may be a "new batch" (v. 7). And this is not something we must do but something we now are—gift, grace: "you really are unleavened." And a little yeast leavens the whole batch of dough.

- Even if you are not a baker, try to imagine how a little yeast leavens a whole batch of dough. How can one, having a new life in Christ, enliven the whole community?

- How does Christ clean us out, clean us up, and make us "unleavened yeast" to become life-giving bread?

23. Decay/Fruit

One could pose "barren" against fruitful, as it is so often used in the Hebrew Bible, but here being barren is not portrayed as the human predicament. The problem is "decay." The good news is the fruit and being able to be fruit-bearing and fruitful. In 2 Thess 2:13 we see that "God chose you as first fruits for salvation . . ." First fruits are grown, but here the verb is *chosen.*

In Phil 1:11 the Christians are described as "having produced the harvest of righteousness that comes through Jesus Christ for the glory and praise of God." In the first chapter of Romans, Paul expresses his desire to visit the believers in Rome "in order that I may reap some harvest among you as I have among the rest of the Gentiles" (1:13). This is in contrast to being "unfruitful" (2 Pet 1:8) and the image of "autumn trees without fruit" (Jude 12). Being fruitful could be growth in the new life in Christ and also growth in the Christian community, the number of those who have become Christians.

Later in Romans, Paul uses the images of "dead to the law" alongside the image of bearing "fruit for death" (Rom 7:5). What does the decay of death look like? Smell like? This is the very absence of life. However, in Rom 7:4 we see the image of having died to the law through the body of Christ, "so that you may belong to another, to him who has been raised from the dead in order that we may bear fruit for God."

In Rom 8:19–23 we have the profound passage about the whole creation, in bondage to decay (v. 21), groaning in labor pains—and "not only the creation, but we ourselves, who have the first fruits of the Spirit, groan inwardly while we wait for the adoption, the redemption of our bodies."

Fruitfulness in juxtaposition to the image of death and decay is put forth clearly in 1 Cor 15:20–23: "But in fact Christ has been raised from the dead, the first fruits of those who have died . . . All will be made alive in Christ. But each in his own order: Christ the first fruits, then at his coming those who belong to Christ." This grace, just like fruit itself, multiplies on the trees and on the vines, as is in the opening to the Letter to the Colossians, referring to the gospel that had come to them: "Just as it is bearing fruit and growing in the whole world, so it has been bearing fruit among yourselves from the day you heard it and truly comprehended the grace of God" (Col 1:6).

This grace we receive is "peaceful fruit" (Heb 12:11), "imperishable" (1 Pet 1:4). We "have been born anew not of perishable, but of imperishable seed" (1 Pet 1:23). Incorporating the image of "dough," in Romans we read, "If the part of the dough offered as first fruits is holy, then the whole batch is holy; and if the root is holy, then the branches also are holy" (11:16). Fruit from the dough offered, fruit from the tree, being in Christ is new, eatable, holy, life-giving. The "fruit of the Spirit is love, joy, peace, patience, kindness, generosity, faithfulness, gentleness, and self-control" (Gal 5:22–23). The image of fruit is the gift of new life and fruit to be shared in Christian living.

- Explore the image of decay. What do you see? Feel? Is it inside? Outside? All around?

- Enjoy the fruitfulness of new life in Christ and the Christian community. Share remembrances of it. Share possibilities for it. Share the fruit!

24. Waterless Places/Life-Giving Waters

Those who live in the desert or the plains may have experienced drought. Most of us have experienced throats parched for water. Around the world people are dying from the lack of water. The human predicament can be like being in a waterless place. How do you image such places? Situations? What is it like to have the promise of water and still have a dry mouth, a dry village, a dry environment?

Although "waterless" is a minor image in the Epistles, Jude's series of images describes intruders who pervert the grace of God. One of the most stark descriptions is this: "They are waterless clouds carried along by the winds" (Jude 12). In contrast, in v. 13 they are described as "wild waves of the sea, casting up the foam of their own shame." In 2 Peter the waterless image is used not in relation to the elements but as a metaphor for harmful people: "These are waterless springs . . ." (2:17).

In James similar words are not about others about whom we should be warned but directed to the reader: "What is your life? For you are a mist that appears for a little while and then vanishes" (4:14).

We are left in deathly dryness. Or we are left with the promise of refreshing mist and clouds that bring rain and then don't. And yet, in the Gospels, in hymns, and certainly in baptism we have the image of grace as the water of new life in which we are cleansed. Look for such images. Look also in this book at Images 30, Unbaptized/Baptized, and Image 50, Stained/Cleansed. Search out the waterless places on the earth still in need and the global efforts to provide wells and life-giving waters. Meanwhile, vocationally, in daily life, people often find themselves in waterless places metaphorically.

Danielle in a Waterless Place

Elaine walks with Danielle and tells her story: "Danielle, a teacher, spoke about her experiences of God's grace, and a friend in her life who gave voice to God's presence in Danielle's situation. She is clearly called by God to her vocation and is well equipped for it in skill and in a joyful personality. She enjoys watching children learn but spoke of the heartbreak: 'When students don't have enough food at home to survive, it pains me, because I want the best for them.' She packs two granola bars each morning, one for her own meal and one for a student who is consistently without food.

"Danielle struggles with other disappointments but she experiences God's grace in her vocation, both in finding her job and in staying there. Although she applied for many locations, she had only one interview. She landed the job, and since then has been working at the same middle school in a small town. Initially, she struggled with the location and the isolation; she had tried to leave for two years, but somehow never did. It seemed like a waterless place. Her friend Rita, a teacher at the high school, pointed to God's presence and activity in Danielle's life: 'Rita is the one who told me that, believing there is something here for me. I believe that God has graced me here because of something that I need to do.'

"Also, just as the Holy Spirit was working in Danielle's life when she was struggling with isolation and wanting to move, so was the Holy Spirit working in her friend Rita when she encouraged Danielle. What Danielle thought was a 'waterless place' came to have 'life-giving waters' in time."

- When have you thirsted for water? When have you felt you were in a waterless place?

- How can the Christ who is the water of new life fill your life where you are and help you care for the earth and its people in need of water and the water of life?

25. Passing Away/Living Forever

This image is central in Christian preaching, teaching, and evangelizing, summed up in an often quoted passage: "For the wages of sin is death, but the free gift of God is eternal life in Christ Jesus our Lord" (Rom 6:23). Many times this is used to accuse or shame an individual to bring him or her to repentance. But the image is broader. "Sin exercised dominion in death, so grace might also exercise dominion through justification leading to eternal life through Jesus Christ our Lord" (Rom 5:21). The human predicament is more than personal. It is societal and systemic. Sin and death were in charge; they reigned. Now, in the resurrection of Christ, justification and eternal life have dominion over everything—in the present, in our daily lives, and into all eternity.

Christ alone has immortality (1 Tim 6:16). Once again we have the image of grace "given to us in Christ Jesus . . . who abolished death and brought life and immortality to light through the gospel" (2 Tim 1:9–10). This living forever is true and sure, as the Letter to Titus begins, "in the hope of eternal life that God, who never lies, promised before the ages began . . ." (1:2).

Other things will pass away: prophecies, speaking in tongues, knowledge, and all things "partial" (1 Cor 13:8–10). Linked to the image of imperishable fruit, we read in 1 Cor 15:35–54 that what is sown is perishable and what is raised is imperishable. The perishable will decay and die with Christ. The perishable body must put on imperishability and the mortal body put on immortality.

The image of grace as living forever is communal, grace "extending to more and more people" (2 Cor 4:15). This communal eternal life is centered in Christ, "because we know that the one who raised the Lord Jesus will raise us also with Jesus, and will bring us with you into his presence" (2 Cor 4:14). And so, the passage continues, "we do not lose heart. Even though our outer nature is wasting away, our inner nature is being renewed day by day."

I spent yesterday afternoon, in the midst of writing this section of the book, with a dear friend, whose body is wasting away from the cancer that is taking over. And yet I did not lose heart, because Thom's inner nature is being renewed day by day, even as he has only weeks, months—who knows—to live. He continues to work on projects for students to prepare them for leadership in global perspectives equating with human rights. He reads, he writes, he speaks to individuals and groups. And his work will go on in perpetuity. Eternal life is a continuation of the new resurrection life begun in our baptisms into the death and resurrection of Christ. "So if anyone is in Christ, there is a new creation: everything old has passed away; see, everything has become new!" (2 Cor 5:17).

Here are two more ways to think of this image: "Our citizenship is in heaven, and it is from there that we are expecting a Savior, the Lord Jesus Christ. He will transform the body of our humiliation that it may be conformed to the body of his glory" (Phil 3:20–21). And from 1 Thess 4:13–18: "We do not want you to be uninformed, brothers and sisters, about those who have died, so that you may not grieve as others do who have no hope. For since we believe that Jesus died and rose again, even so, through Jesus, God will bring with him those who have died. . . . Therefore encourage one another with these words."

Michael the Funeral Home Director

The story of Janine's walk with Michael: "Michael warmly greeted me as I entered the funeral home located in a small country town. He was there early to attend to the last-minute details, care for the body, put on the wig, wait for the flowers and then for the guests to arrive. I observed that it is the funeral director who sets the mood and the tone of the funeral.

"Michael shared that the challenges that he faces range from the laws and regulations for the funeral industry to having limited resources and space to hold a funeral that is fitting and appropriate. For instance, there is a body in the holding room that has been embalmed and is awaiting burial or cremation but the absence of a will and close relatives has caused the matter to be tied up in the courts for weeks.

"Michael emphasized that being a funeral director is not an occupation, or a job: it is his calling. He serves God by serving others and treats each individual as made in the image of God. Michael is sensitive toward how various cultures grieve. Hispanics will wail together in groups. Their lamenting will often last longer and be surrounded by times of prayer. African Americans wail also, but usually one at a time. They sometimes have a more flexible time schedule. When Michael meets with a family who is struggling over the planning, he reminds them that nothing is urgent. Their loved one has already died and the family has time to think about how their loved one would have wanted their funeral.

"Michael talked about walking with people during their difficult times. It involves picking up bodies in the middle of the night, sitting in family meetings, listening and guiding the family dynamics. These are the difficult parts of the job. It is more than wearing the nice suit and driving a nice vehicle. Michael is a minister to people as they grieve the loss of their loved ones. It is a vocation about which he is passionate.

"Michael asserted that the word *funeral* is a misnomer. It is a celebration of life and an integral part of a needed grieving process. Funerals used to be two to three days long, but over the years they have become shorter. Michael explained how he gives people the opportunity to understand the importance of the final viewing and saying goodbye, the ability to see their loved one after the body is made up. Since people are living longer, there are many instances when the loved one has been 'gone' before death. Therefore, memories may have been from recent illness or years of illness. The viewing can help the family recall their loved one as she was in her vitality and not as she was in recent years when sick or gripped by dementia.

"Michael pays attention to the spiritual and emotional needs of the whole person. People no longer recognize God in the midst of it all, Michael commented. In the midst of death and sadness, what gives Michael hope? His hope comes from being certain in the promise of everlasting life and living out what God called him to be. Addressing issues of grief are Michael's way of sharing God's boundless love with the world. We dare to hope in the promise of the resurrection, not on the basis of what we do in our lives or our professions, but because of what God has done for us in and through Christ Jesus!"

- Immortality and eternal life are the free gifts of grace through Jesus Christ. What questions and certainties do you hold about this new life that begins here and never ends?

- How do you grieve? How can we help each other gain skill in helping others grieve well?

CHAPTER 4

From Alienation to Belonging

We begin this chapter with the very human reality of the many ways people experience alienation and the grace of God in Christ, who calls us to belong to him and therefore to one another. Some of us have experienced being exiled. The good news is that in Christ God has chosen the exiled. Likewise, there are many ways in which people are disinherited. For them the image of becoming heirs is good news. Estrangement is so painful; estrangement from God feels so ultimate. God not only invites human beings back but invites them back as partners. The sacrament of baptism is an entry into the community. Here it is also an image of belonging. Throughout the Epistles one sees Christian communities torn apart in division. The gift of grace is unity, not just so that the gospel might be preached, but as gospel itself. Three minor images provide ways to picture belonging: becoming God's people rather than "not my people," being grafted onto the tree rather than broken off, and being God's house rather than merely a servant who does not belong. All of these images are in their own ways expressions of the good news of belonging to Christ and, through Christ, to one another.

26. Alienation/Belonging

In Ephesians we have the haunting words, "Remember that you were at that time without Christ, being aliens from the commonwealth of Israel, and strangers to the covenants of promise, having no hope and without God in the world" (2:12). To be without Christ is to be alienated from community. Now, one could challenge the assumption that to be outside the community of Christ is to have no community—all major religions have a community of believers. All people form communities of some kind. However, the reality remains that in today's world people experience all kinds of estrangement and alienation. "Belonging" is an essential element of being in Christ. It is not just an element of grace; it *is* grace, unconditional acceptance and relationship with God and human beings and the creation itself.

Alienation brings loneliness, loss of hope in one's life. The Christian gift is inclusion. Because being united is a gift, Christians are called to live this out in their daily relationships.

Rosemary's Alienation

Here is Deanna's story of her walk with Rosemary: "I met with Rosemary at her home on a Sunday after worship. She attended a church today that she has not been attending for a few years because she was offended by the pastor there. But this day was different. She attended church again to welcome the new pastor into the community.

"Neither of us had eaten before I arrived, so she looked in her refrigerator and found some sandwich makings and some cookies and ice cream. She said she wanted to change her clothes and get into something more comfortable, explaining that getting older keeps her from being able to dress up like she used to, with nylons and heels. Right there I saw the first and probably biggest human predicament for her—her physical limitations due to the aging process. She said that being eighty-two years old really keeps her from doing as much as she used to. She is no longer able to play golf, which was one of her ways of keeping active physically.

"As we visited over lunch, I felt as if we were just a couple of girls taking refuge from the wet and cold outdoors to share a cup of hot apple cider and working to solve all the problems of the world in one afternoon. Rosemary lives alone in the home she and her husband built at the top of a bluff that looks out over the Mississippi River. The view is amazing and inspiring, but her story was equally inspiring for me. We talked about the joys of grandchildren and great grandchildren, and we talked about the sadness of death. Her youngest son was killed by a hit-and-run driver sixteen years ago, and her husband died of an aneurism ten years ago. About a year ago, she learned that her oldest son had been diagnosed with lymphoma, and ten days after his diagnosis, his wife was diagnosed with breast cancer. In the midst of all this tragedy, Rosemary has remained engaged in community activities. She is a petite woman packed with energy and enthusiasm. Even though she had become disheartened with church services, this past week she had welcomed the new pastor into her home as a houseguest while he was in town preparing for his family to move here. She and I visited for nearly three hours about nothing, and yet about everything.

"In Rosemary's world, people have always thought that her family and her life were 'perfect.' Rosemary was married to a banker and they raised four children. She told me about the big home they lived in when the children were still young. My family lived in poverty, and yet through our conversation I began to understand that the same 'world' existed in their family as did in my family. Because of the secretive abuse going on in our home, there were never friends 'hanging out' or spending time at our house. But the same kind of secret was happening in Rosemary's home. Most people were not aware of mental illness issues back in the seventies, and so most people didn't know about her son's condition. My world of secrets didn't seem to be much different than her world of secrets. Separation and alienation are realities for those with 'secrets.' Her family life was an image of perfection, even though it has been far from perfection.

"Rosemary has suffered significant losses in her life. The move with her husband to her current home after her children had grown and married away didn't bring about as much loneliness as her husband's death did. That left her alone in this big house in a community so far away from her family. Sometimes the pain of loss can run so deep that it alienates us from those who have given us the comfort of company. Rosemary experienced this same type of alienation when she left the church because of something that was said by the pastor shortly after her husband died.

"It is important as the community of God's children to share with each other what God is doing and where God is with us in our journey together. We can empower others with their gifts to share God's love with their neighbor. In Jesus Christ we experience the belonging of God's participation in our lives."

Offense, Alienation, and Belonging

First Corinthians 10:23–33 concludes with these words: "So, whether you eat or drink, or whatever you do, do everything for the glory of God. Give no offense to Jews or to Greeks or to the church of God, just as I try to please everyone in everything I do, not seeking my own advantage, but that of many, so that they may be saved" (vv. 31–33). The Epistles themselves testify that even in the midst of our giving offense to one another and our many ways of becoming alienated, the gift of Christ Jesus is unconditional love eternally with God and with one another. For example, in 1 John 1:3, we read, "We declare to you what we have seen and heard so that you also may have fellowship with us; and truly our fellowship is with the Father and with his Son Jesus Christ."

Many passages in the Epistles provide a strong basis for the unity Christians have in Christ, some of which will be explored in other images in this chapter. Romans 8:31–39 may be the most powerful. God did not withhold God's own Son, but "gave him up for all of us" (v. 32). God justifies. Christ died and was raised. "Who will separate us from the love of Christ? Will hardship, or distress, or persecution, or famine, or nakedness, or peril or sword? . . . I am convinced that neither death, nor life, nor angels, nor rulers, nor things present, nor things to come, nor powers, nor height, nor depth, nor anything else in all creation, will be able to separate us from the love of God in Christ Jesus our Lord" (vv. 38–39). The cross and resurrection are about never again being separated from God or, since these verses are persistently plural, from one another. This unity is grace.

These various images within an image say consistent things: the Christ event is about becoming and belonging in Christ. Each of us has been and can become alienated and estranged. In Christ we belong. Therefore, it is appropriate to conclude with 2 Cor 10:7—"If you are confident that you belong to Christ, remind yourself of this, that just as you belong to Christ, so also do we . . ."—and Rom 15:7: "Welcome one another, therefore, just as Christ has welcomed you, for the glory of God."

- When and from whom have you experienced alienation? What were the causes?

- How do people become estranged from a faith community, even as the community does not realize it? How can we become more aware of this early on, rather than later?

- How does the grace of Jesus Christ give us the gift of belonging, even while we are yet alienated from one another? How can we make this real for people?

27. Exiled/Chosen

Some of us have had the experience of being exiled from a country, from an ethnic group, from a church body; some have not. The Hebrew Bible carries the story of a people in exile. It is our story. And in New Testament times, Peter addresses the "exiles of the Dispersion in Pontus, Galatia, Cappadocia, Asia, and Bithynia" (1 Pet 1:1), calling them in general "exiles and aliens" (1 Pet 2:11). In one's personal story, one can experience, for a short time or for a lifetime, being exiled from one's family or community. When one must live in a strange land, not among one's own people, feeling lonely and perhaps even exiled from God, the good news is that we have been chosen.

The Epistle to the Ephesians begins with the now familiar words, "Grace to you and peace from God," and specifically, "Blessed be the God and Father of our Lord Jesus Christ, who has blessed us in Christ with every spiritual blessing in the heavenly places, just as he chose us in Christ before the foundation of the world to be holy and blameless before him in love" (1:2-4). This choseness is "redemption" and "forgiveness" and "grace" that God "lavished on us." We have been "adopted" through Jesus Christ, according to God's good will (Eph 1:5-8). The grace of being chosen children!

Similarly, 1 Thessalonians begins with the image of grace as being chosen. The "brothers and sisters" are called "beloved of God" and said to have been chosen because the message of the gospel came to them "not in word only, but also in power and in the Holy Spirit and with full conviction" (1:4-5). And in 2 Thessalonians we read, "But we must always give thanks to God for you, brothers and sisters beloved by the Lord, because God chose you as the first fruits for salvation through sanctification by the Spirit and through belief in the truth" (2:13). The exiles and aliens in the letter of First Peter are said to have been "chosen and destined by God the Father and sanctified by the Sprit to be obedient to Jesus Christ and to be sprinkled with his blood" (1:1). No longer exiled—now, through Christ, chosen!

- What do you understand, from history or from your own story, about being in exile? What does it mean? What are the consequences—for the present and for the future?

- How have you experienced being a chosen child? How does—or might—your faith community live in grace realizing that by grace you have been chosen? What might that mean for mission to those beyond your own people?

28. Disinherited/Heirs

Ephesians 3:6 makes clear what is a radical concept in Acts and in the Epistles: Gentiles now become fellow heirs with those of Jewish heritage, members of Christ's body and "sharers in the promise in Christ Jesus through the gospel." Once again inclusivity is directly rooted in the gospel itself.

So what does being "heirs" imply? In the first chapter of Ephesians inheritance is specifically mentioned: "In Christ we have . . . obtained an inheritance" (v. 11) and it is connected once again to hope and "the gospel of salvation" (v. 13). Also, in verse 18 we have the phrase "the riches of [Christ's] glorious inheritance among the saints." Likewise, Titus 3:6–7 shows becoming "heirs according to the hope of eternal life." This is not a prosperity gospel but "justification by grace," which the Spirit "poured out on us richly through Jesus Christ our Savior."

In Gal 3:29, which follows the profound statement in verse 28 that there is no longer Jew or Greek, slave or free, male or female, "for all of you are one in Christ Jesus," we read, "If you belong to Christ, then you are Abraham's offspring, heirs according to the promise." "Heir" and "promise" are central, and belonging is always "in Christ Jesus." Salvation is belonging to Christ, and that always comes with belonging to the other; and that "other" shares the inheritance, the promise. That "other" is the one from whom we may be the most alienated: the stranger, by the world's calculation.

Chris at United Way's 211 Hotline

Kelsey tells the following story of her walk with Chris: "I spent my day with Chris, who is the manager for United Way's 211 Hotline in a midsize city. We began our day at the office downtown, a new building built after the floods five years ago. The beautiful building sits deliberately in a difficult part of town against the railroad tracks.

"Chris took me around to meet everyone in the office, from the director to the interns, saying, 'Kelsey's spending the day with me to learn about my calling.' Chris and I then traveled together to the offices where the 211 hotline operates twenty-four hours a day, seven days a week. The supervisor, Sandy, told me that among the myriad agencies to whom they refer people, very few are churches. Some churches have food pantries, but they are well known and usually at max capacity for food requests. I asked, 'If there was one thing you could ask from churches to help people in need, what would it be?' Without hesitation Sandy replied, 'Rental assistance or transportation.'

"Sandy explained that many people who call 211 live on the edge of financial disaster, literally disinherited in every sense. They must pick and choose which bills to pay. Rental assistance helps people on that edge make it until the next month, and perhaps that will help them break the cycle. That is the hope.

"Transportation is a key hardship, too. People who have a loved one die out of state and need to travel for a funeral are often unable to travel. People may have moved and want to return to their home area. People sometimes move to rural areas because the rent there is reasonable, but public transportation in most rural areas is virtually nonexistent for people under the age of sixty-five.

"At lunch together, Chris and I talked about her call to her work at the United Way. She loved the theme of her church body's[1] twenty-fifth anniversary, 'God's Work, Our Hands.' Our nation feeds, financially supports, educates, and houses people in need. We do this through government programs and charitable giving. At the same time, there is often a feeling of disgusted pity for the people who receive such services. There are those among us who see people in need as outsiders, unable to 'get their act together.' I overheard a man at breakfast the other day saying that if 'people are hungry enough they'll get a job.'

"Chris sees every person as an heir, and through the vision of the cross she does not lose hope. Her Christian imagination is alive and well and impacting meetings, programs, and people. I want to be just like her! I will pray for generosity of heart and sincerity in hospitality. I will hope each day that even the man I overheard at breakfast trying to starve people out of

---

1. The Evangelical Lutheran Church in America

poverty will be made new in Christ. I will focus through worship and practice on the cross of Christ, which propels us forward into the world so that we nearly tumble out the doors of the church to love. I will know Christ."

Heirs through Adoption

The image of belonging and being an heir includes being "adopted." Galatians 4:1–7 entwines heir, adoption, and enslavement. The comparison from that first-century world is that heirs who are minors are "no better than slaves, though they are owners of all the property," for they need a guardian. In the fullness of time, Jesus was "born of a woman, born under the law, in order to redeem those who were under the law, so that we might receive adoption as children" (vv. 4–5). And so, the comparison goes, "you are no longer a slave but a child, and if a child then also an heir, through God" (v. 7). Belonging in twenty-first-century terms might be spelled out in different ways. But, once again, Christ and his incarnation are central to bringing about belonging. We do not see the image of "family" prominent here. Congregations that refer to themselves as "family" churches may be unintentionally alienating some people who do not belong to a traditional family or do not see themselves fitting into *this* particular family. Our belonging in Christ as adopted children, as alienated strangers, as heirs by grace alone is a more radical and real concept.

In Romans we see the image of adoption in a number of ways. Romans 8:23 states that "we wait for adoption, the redemption of our bodies." In Rom 9:3–5, Paul's anguish and love for "his own people" who have not accepted Christ leads him to say that he wishes he could be "cut off from Christ" for the sake of his own people. "They are Israelites, and to them belong the adoption, the glory . . . the promises . . ." This could lead us to explore the question of whether God rejects people. Paul answers, "By no means!" (Rom 11:1). All of this raises the issue of mission to those who were insiders at one time as well as to those who have not previously been included. There is always the possibility of those who have separated themselves being included once again.

- What inheritance have you received? Or not received? How prominent a place does being an heir or receiving an inheritance play in your life?

- What might it mean to think about belonging to Christ in terms of being an heir of salvation? What does such an inheritance mean in relation to all of your other possessions?

29. Estranged/Partners

Who has not known the pain of being separated from those one loves? In which situation does one suffer more—in being apart from a beloved, or in being estranged when a relationship is broken? Each is differently difficult. And what does it feel like to be estranged from God?

We *are* estranged from God and from one another. This may be the essence of sin, the human predicament. Jesus the Christ experienced such suffering in being estranged from his own religious leaders, separated from his family, deserted by his disciples, and finally forsaken by God on the cross. Being estranged from one another as human beings is so difficult to overcome. Reconciliation—new relationships—is the work of God. The image is expressed this way in Colossians: "And you who were once estranged and hostile in mind, doing evil deeds, he [Christ] has now reconciled in his fleshly body through death . . ." (1:21–22). Jesus becomes the mediator among the estranged: "there is one God: there is also one mediator between God and humankind, Christ Jesus, himself human . . ." (1 Tim 2:5).

Often in the Epistles, messengers of the gospel are called partners and coworkers. Paul refers to Titus as "my partner and coworker in your service" (2 Cor 8:23). This separation and partnership image is found throughout the book of Philemon. Onesimus and Philemon were separated by miles but also by the institution of slavery. Paul appeals to Philemon—saying frankly, "if you consider me your partner" (v. 17)—to receive Onesimus back "no longer as a slave but more than a slave, a beloved brother—especially to me but how much more to you, both in the flesh and in the Lord" (Phil 16).

Those linked together in Christ are now brothers and sisters, as is affirmed in the opening of many of the Epistles—for example, "We must always give thanks to God for you, brothers and sisters . . ." (2 Thess 1:3). And again and again, the writers of the Letters express their pain at being apart. In 1 Thess 2:17, the writer is "orphaned" from "brothers and sisters": "As for us, brothers and sisters, when, for a short time, we were made orphans by being separated from you—in person, not in heart—we longed with great eagerness to see you face to face."

Being partners, not separated or estranged, comes through the grace of God, and is mutual: "It is right for me to think this way about all of you, because you hold me in your heart, for all of you share in God's grace with me, both in my imprisonment and in the defense and confirmation of the gospel. For God is my witness, how I long for all of you with the compassion of Christ Jesus" (Phil 1:7–8). The commendations at the conclusion of the Letters also attest to the new bonds of relationship in Christ (e.g., Rom 16). And even though human bonds are broken again and again, the good news is that in Christ estrangement from God is no longer ultimate. We look again at Rom 8:35–39, this time focusing on the first and last verses: "Who will separate us from the love of Christ?" and nothing "will be able to separate us from the love of God in Christ Jesus our Lord."

- From whom have you been estranged? For a short while or for years? In what ways have you felt estranged from God? Consider that Christ, who suffered estrangement himself, knows how you feel. How does being a partner with Christ change all our relationships even while we are still living in the midst of human predicaments?

- What partnerships in Christ do you cherish? How might you give thanks for them? Build on them?

Tanner at the Coffee Pub

Dave sees Tanner's daily work as vocation. He writes, "Tanner serves coffee at the Coffee Pub. Sometimes we have long conversations; other times he is too busy to interact much. He is in his late forties or early fifties. Tanner has experienced great pain in his life. He was married once and is now divorced. Tanner takes great pride in his work. He battles carpal tunnel to keep a grip on what he has to do all day.

"Tanner's day is filled with a diverse revolving assembly who gather at the pub: those who are single, dating, those who are broken and those seemingly whole. I have seen law enforcement and people recovering from hangovers at the same bar. Some are passing through for the first time; some are regulars and some in a hurry. Those who stay a while work on computers, read newspapers, or make small talk. Others are silent. There is a variety of clothing styles, tattoos, political views, and more. Yet here, everyone is important. Tanner is interested in your life. He knows people's stories, the good and the painful.

"I don't think Tanner sees his daily work as vocation. In fact he is skeptical about the church, remembering only judgment and condemnation, another of the scars from his past. The gospel message has been lost on account of the messenger. Tanner respects the church; he is concerned about social issues. Tanner welcomes the alienated, the estranged, and serves them. He greets them by name and has watched some of the young people grow up. He lives in a way that promotes community and belonging, even partnership among diversity. People choose to come here rather than staying isolated and alienated at home. Here milk and water are transformed into lattes, coffee, and tea. A kaleidoscope of social needs are contained in cups of all sizes. One morning the talk was of the shooting of two teens in the neighborhood.

"There's a pattern to Tanner's work. He fills the bottle cooler, left barren from the night before. He grinds new batches of fresh organic beans and brews again and again. Tanner also cleans the dishes and tools of his trade. He cleans the bathroom, messes he didn't make. He is presider and custodian all in one. The gospel is a message of hope that reaches out into our communities, to coffee bars and street corners. I need to learn the languages of these places so I can recognize and speak to people in meaningful ways that proclaim the resurrection hope."

30. Unbaptized/Baptized

Baptism is a sacrament of the church; in this book we see it also as an image of the grace of God in Jesus Christ. The two are directly connected. "As many of you as were baptized in Christ have clothed yourselves with Christ" (Gal 3:27). This is followed immediately by verse 28 proclaiming that baptism is not private but always communal, always uniting those who otherwise might be alienated from one another: "There is no longer Jew or Greek, there is no longer slave or free, there is no longer male or female; for all of you are one in Christ Jesus." Likewise, at the conclusion of the 1 Corinthians body of Christ passage, we read, "For in the one Spirit we were all baptized into one body—Jews or Greeks, slaves or free—and we were all made to drink of one Spirit" (12:13). All who have been baptized belong to Christ—together.

As with each of these images, this image, too, is directly connected with the saving work of the death and resurrection of Christ: "But when the goodness and loving kindness of God our Savior appeared, he saved us, not because of any works of righteousness that we had done, but according to his mercy, through the water of rebirth and renewal by the Holy Spirit. This Spirit he poured out on us richly through Jesus Christ our Savior . . ." (Titus 3:4–6).

So, what about the unbaptized? Paul in 1 Corinthians contrasts in descriptive terms their lives before their baptism, the human predicament of "what some of you used to be." It would be presumptuous for us to describe unbaptized people in those terms. The words that follow, however, are bold and true: "But you were washed, you were sanctified, you were justified in the name of the Lord Jesus Christ and in the Spirit of our God" (6:11). First Peter also refers to baptism as washing, but not ordinary cleansing: "And baptism . . . now saves you—not as a removal of dirt from the body, but as an appeal to God for a good conscience, through the resurrection of Jesus Christ" (3:21).

"Do you not know that all of us who have been baptized into Christ Jesus were baptized into his death? Therefore we have been buried with him by baptism into death, so that, just as Christ was raised from the dead by the glory of the Father, so we too might walk in newness of life" (Rom 6:3–4). In the sacrament of baptism each person enters into the death and resurrection of Christ. This is an image, yet more than an image.

Too many times the location of a baptism, who attends, what those in attendance choose to wear, and even who baptizes become the focal points. Paul addresses that very issue to a divided church in Corinth in these stark words: "Has Christ been divided? . . . Or were you baptized in the name of Paul? I thank God that I baptized none of you except Crispus and Gaius, so that no one can say that you were baptized in my name. (I did baptize also the household of Stephanas; beyond that, I do not know whether I baptized anyone else.)" (1 Cor 1:13–16). These rather informal, almost random comments seem somewhat out of place in Holy Scripture, but this is a letter, written to specific people in a specific situation. One cannot take a verse out of place and use it as a proof text in general. For example, "For Christ did not send me to baptize but to proclaim the gospel" (1 Cor 1:17a) cannot be interpreted to mean that preaching is more important than sacraments. One must go on to read the rest of the verse, which also illumines the whole section: "so that the cross of Christ might not be emptied of its power" (1 Cor 1:17b). In being baptized we belong to Christ, his cross and resurrection, and they are powerful in our daily lives in the world.

- Have you been baptized? If so, what do you remember about that day, or what have you been told? How was the whole church, global and historic, present among the people that day?

- What does being buried with Christ in his death and being risen with Christ in his resurrection mean for your ministry in daily life in the death and life struggles you face? You belong to Christ.

31. Division/Unity

Throughout the centuries divisions have plagued the church. Paul makes clear in the 1 Cor 1:10–17 passage mentioned in the previous section that we cannot say, "I belong to Cephas" or "I belong to Apollos," because Christ cannot be divided (v. 13). Chapter 3 of 1 Corinthians describes the divisions (as do many other parts of the Epistles), often by saying people "belong" to one or another church leader. It is clear that these divisions are not to be, and we cannot save ourselves through them or from them. We all belong to Christ and Christ belongs to God. Being together in Christ is a central salvation theme.

Included in moving from alienation to belonging through Christ's incarnation, death, and resurrection is the image of living in division and the grace of being united in Christ. The three passages on the image of the body of Christ—Rom 12, 1 Cor 12 (which really begins with 1 Cor 11), and Eph 4—are central. However, let us start by considering others.

In Eph 2:14 we read that Christ "is our peace; in his flesh he has made both groups into one and has broken down the dividing wall, that is, the hostility between us." This section, Eph 2:11–17, is pertinent to many images in this chapter. In verse 16 we see that Christ reconciles "both groups to God in one body through the cross, thus putting to death that hostility through it."

Christ unites even across generations. The reference in 1 Cor 10:1–5 is to the exodus of the Israelites. "They drank from the spiritual rock that followed them, and the rock was Christ" (v. 4). The letter goes on to say that God was not pleased with most of them; however, Christ being central is noteworthy.

Some church bodies have taken 2 Cor 6:14ff. as a proof text for keeping themselves divided from others who do not believe precisely as they do: "Do not be mismatched with unbelievers." This is an unfortunate use of this one verse. On the other hand, four chapters of the Pauline Epistles provide a strong basis for the unity Christians have in Christ: Rom 12, 1 Cor 11 and 12, and Eph 4.

Rom 12

The middle verses, 4–8, are often pulled out to show the different gifts in the body of Christ and, at times, to make a case for hierarchical leadership. But here, as in 1 Cor 12 and Eph 4, the lists are open and not ranked. The church is not the extraneous wrapping; the church is the gift of grace itself. God transforms and renews lest anyone think oneself more significant than another (v. 3). In the one body are many members, each with its own function: "For as in one body we have many members, and not all the members have the same function, so we, who are many, are one body in Christ, and individually we are members one of another" (v. 4). As in the human body, no member functions when it is divided from the others.

The remainder of the chapter describes how love needs to be genuine and what that love will look like: "love one another with mutual affection; outdo one another in showing honor . . . extend hospitality to strangers" (vv. 9–13).

1 Cor 11:17–34

God will not let anything keep us divided, but human beings will find ways to perpetuate divisions. Paul says, "For, to begin with, when you come together as a church, I hear that there are divisions among you; and to some extent I believe it" (v. 18). These "factions" (v. 19) are particularly grievous at the Lord's Supper: "Each of you goes ahead with your own supper, and one goes hungry and another becomes drunk" (v. 21). Then we have the passage that is used to this day globally for the institution of the Lord's Supper: "This is my body that is for you . . ." (vv. 23–26).

The verses immediately following have been quoted by church bodies who wish to keep Christians not of their "body" (denomination) away from their table, and to keep their own members away if they are not worthy through specific "examination": "Whoever, therefore, eats the bread or drinks the cup of the Lord in an unworthy manner will be answerable for the body and blood of the Lord. Examine yourselves, and only then eat of the bread and drink of the cup" (vv. 27–28). The trump card is played with the following verse: "For all who eat and drink without discerning the body, eat and drink judgment against themselves" (v.29).

With this one verse people have been kept from union with the body of Christ at the table. Others have kept themselves from union through fear, thinking, "Maybe I don't feel guilty enough," or "Maybe I have not memorized enough Bible passages," or "Maybe I don't have the correct interpretation of the meaning of the Lord's Supper." But where are these ideas in 1 Cor 11? "Not discerning the body" clearly relates to factions, to division between rich and poor and whatever other divisions Christians cause among themselves. The passage began with, and ends with, this message of inclusivity. "So then, my brothers and sisters, when you come together to eat, wait for one another. If you are hungry, eat at home, so that when you come together, it will not be for your condemnation" (vv. 33–34). To be, to cause, to remain in division is the opposite of the gift Christians are to receive at the table: union with Christ in his body and within the body, among all Christians.

1 Cor 12:1–31

The naming of individual gifts and activities could be (has been) used to cause divisions in the church. Clarity of roles is important, but there is one united community in Christ. One's identity is in Christ, not in one's role (e.g., ordained pastoral ministry). The gift of union in Christ is at the core: the same Spirit, the same Lord, and the same God (vv. 4–6). "For just as the body is one and has many members, and all the members of the body, though many, are one body, so it is with Christ. For in the one Spirit we were all baptized into one body—Jews or Greeks, slaves or free—and we were all made to drink of one Spirit" (vv. 12–13).

As important as the first thirteen verses of the chapter are, those that follow are perhaps more important: the gift of grace in Christ is the union in the body. People, in their self-doubt, may think they are not needed, but that does not keep God from the work of uniting. "If the foot would say, 'Because I am not a hand, I do not belong to the body,' that would not make it any less a part of the body" (v. 15). The concept is repeated lest one miss the point: "And if the ear would say, 'Because I am not an eye, I do not belong to the body,' that would not make it any less a part of the body" (v. 16).

Human beings may thoughtlessly or purposely try to divide the body, but uniting in Christ's body is God's work and cannot be undone: "The eye cannot say to the hand, 'I have no need of you,' nor again the head to the feet, 'I have no need of you'" (v. 21).[2] The weaker are indispensable. The less honorable are clothed (vv. 22–23).[3] If one suffers, all suffer; if one member is honored, all rejoice together (v. 26).

Then, but only then, follows the passage concerning the appointments in the church (vv. 27–30)—prefaced by the words, "Now you are the body of Christ and individually members of it"—whichs lead right into v. 31 and chapter 13, on love.

Eph 4:1–16

Christians are called to make every effort to maintain that which is already a gift: the unity of the Spirit in the bond of peace (v. 3). Once again we see there is one body, one Spirit, one hope, one Lord, one faith, one baptism, one God (vv. 4–6). We see the gifts and hear the call. The various gifts are given not for division into rankings, but "to equip the saints for the work of ministry, for building up the body of Christ" (v. 12).

The members "must no longer be children, tossed to and fro and blown about by every wind of doctrine, by people's trickery, by their craftiness in deceitful scheming" (v. 14), all of which are ways human beings would divide themselves once more. But "speaking the truth in love, we must grow up in every way into him who is the head, into Christ, from whom the whole body, joined and knit together by every ligament with which it is equipped, as each part is working properly, promotes the body's growth in building itself up in love" (vv. 15–16).

The body of Christ passages are such central salvation images—Christ incarnate, Christ's body on the cross, Christ's resurrected body, and Christ's body given in the Eucharist.

- What church divisions have you experienced—given you pain, caused whole communities to hurt one another, become alienated, dysfunctional, broken? What were the results?

- How is unity in Christ a gift? A gift of grace and salvation in Christ itself?

2. Note that although Christ is the "head of the body" in most body of Christ images, here the head is simply one of the members. It is as if in this discourse that concept is more important.

3. Note the unclothed/clothed minor image later in chapter 7.

- How have you been and how are you being strengthened, empowered, and equipped to become part of the healing rather than part of the dividing of Christ's church?

32. Not a People/God's People

"I'm a nobody" people sometimes say of themselves. Whole families or peoples sometimes undervalue themselves. However, to be called "not a people" by God carried the designation to a whole other level. Perhaps even worse than judgment—when one is at least seen—is being not acknowledged at all. First Peter refers to the prophet Hosea[4] in using the image: "Once you were not a people, but now you are God's people; once you had not received mercy, but now you have received mercy" (2:10).

Paul too quotes Hosea,[5] now including not only Jews but also Gentiles: "Those who were not my people I will call 'my people,' and her who was not beloved I will call 'beloved.' And in the very place where it was said to them, 'You are not my people,' there they shall be called children of the living God" (Rom 9:25–26).

Hebrews contains a significant passage about God making a new covenant with God's people and uses this image as well: "And I will be their God, and they shall be my people" (8:10). The state of being alienated, being named a "no one," is transformed through Christ into forever belonging to God's own self.

- When have you felt, even for a short time, that you were a nobody? What did that feel like? What were the consequences?

- What does it feel like to be acknowledged by name? To be named by God? To be claimed by God as belonging to God forever?

Bill the Firefighter and Pig Farmer

Miguel walks with Bill and tells this story: "Bill is a full-time firefighter and a part-time pig farmer. We spent time together on his farm while I listened to his story. He grew up in the area and went to technical college. He and

4. Hos 1:9: "Then the LORD said, 'Name him [the child] Lo-ammi, for you are not my people and I am not your God.'"

5. Hos 1:10: ". . . and in the place where it was said to them, 'You are not my people,' it shall be said to them, 'Children of the living God.'"

his wife have lived on the same farm since they were married thirty years ago; they have two children, now grown.

"While his children were growing up he would attend church on occasion. His work schedule with the fire department didn't allow him to attend on a regular basis. He admitted he could have gone more often but used the work schedule as an excuse. Bill didn't pinpoint the reason, but seemed wary of church because he didn't really see faith as influencing or being a part of his everyday work. Bill's wife would faithfully take their two children to Sunday school and worship every Sunday.

"As the children grew older, they were relatively involved in the church, and Bill's daughter began working for the church part-time as the youth director after college. His children's excitement for the church seemed to be what encouraged Bill to attend more often. It seemed as if he was gradually easing back. He slowly began serving on committees, taught Sunday school, and recently was elected president of the church council. There was room in this church for someone whom others rarely saw as part of the people to once again become a central part of the people of God in this place.

"During my second visit with Bill, I helped with some work in the field. Afterwards we had lunch together and talked about his work with the fire department. It involves more than fighting fires. They are called to all 911 scenes and typically serve as EMTs. Bill is a contemplative person, one who considers the purpose and realities of life. Both at the farm and the fire station he observes life and death firsthand. He sees it as a privilege to help people in their difficult times.

"In talking about his work as a farmer, he said he was most proud of the neighborhood teenagers who helped on the farm as he watched them grow into responsible adults. He said, 'The best crop I ever grew were those boys.' He spoke in the same way about the new recruits at the fire station. He also spoke fondly of the young people at church with whom he was beginning to become involved.

"As I considered Bill's life, I could see how his faith has influenced his everyday life, even if he didn't realize it. He now connects his faith with his life and speaks about it and about God's people, seeking to bring a healing presence into the lives of those he encounters."

33. Broken Off/Grafted Onto the Tree

"And even those of Israel, if they do not persist in unbelief, will be grafted in, for God has the power to graft them in again. For if you have been cut from what is by nature a wild olive tree and grafted, contrary to nature, into a cultivated olive tree, how much more will these natural branches be grafted back into their own olive tree" (Rom 11:23–24). Paul, who considers himself an apostle to the Gentiles, is speaking to Gentile Christians: "For if their rejection is the reconciliation of the world, what will their acceptance be but life from the dead!" (Rom 11:15); just a verse later he says, "if the root is holy, then the branches also are holy" (v. 16)

One needs to be careful not to use this section of Romans to minimize the dangers of anti-Judaism or to start a campaign to convert present-day adherents of the Jewish faith to Christianity, citing, for example, verse 20, "They were broken off because of their unbelief," as an argument. Paul reminds the Gentile Christians, "But if some of the branches were broken off, and you, a wild olive shoot, were grafted in their place to share the rich root of the olive tree, do not boast over the branches . . . remember that it is not you that support the root, but the root that supports you" (vv. 17–18).

- Think of the varieties of ways in which you may have been "broken off"—from community, from relationships, or from God's very self.

- How does God in Jesus Christ "graft" us (sometimes wild olive branches) back onto the tree? Take the image in other directions: What is the root? What is the tree of life?

34. A Servant in the House/The House Itself

"Home sweet home." "There's no place like home." Countless phrases conjure up images of being at home, but what if one's dwelling does not feel like home? What if the house where one spends each night is a place where one does not belong? What if one is a servant in the house? Now, there are many home care workers for whom the use of their gifts and their energy to care for the people in the house or the house itself is their vocation. That is a very good thing. However, the image here is that of being merely a servant, a slave, an outsider, alienated from the ones who really "belong" in the house. The image of grace in the Epistles is that those made saints through the work of Christ are "members of the household of God, built upon the foundation of the apostles and prophets, with Christ Jesus himself as the cornerstone" (Eph 2:19–20). The passage goes on, "In him the whole structure is joined together and grows into a holy temple in the Lord; in whom you also are built together spiritually into a dwelling place for God" (vv. 21–22). Picture that!

The Letter to the Hebrews uses this image to contrast Jesus with Moses, saying that "Moses was faithful in all God's house as a servant. . . . Christ, however, was faithful over God's house as a son, and we are his house if we hold firm the confidence and the pride that belong to hope" (3:5–6). And finally, "Come to him, a living stone, though rejected by mortals yet chosen and precious in God's sight, and like living stones, let yourselves be built into a spiritual house . . ." (1 Pet 2:4–5). God builds us together with the rejected stone, Christ, into a new spiritual house.

- Imagine yourself and others belonging to Christ as a house, with Christ as the cornerstone. Picture being not just inhabitants but the very household of God. Expand this image. What might it mean for stewardship, faithfulness, mission, and inclusivity?

- How do you live as the household of God with doors and windows open to the world?

CHAPTER 5

Called Out of Meaninglessness for Purpose

Whether the problem is boredom or busyness, a sense of meaninglessness sometimes creeps into people's lives; it is a common manifestation of the human predicament. God's call is not just a result of grace but the embodiment of grace. We are called from futility to purposeful service, from uselessness to the full use of our varied gifts of grace for vocation in daily life. At a deeper level people struggle to believe that they and their lives are of value; however, Christ has bought us, redeemed us, saved us from needing to earn our own worth.

Christ has become our obedience when we feel the burden of disobedience. When we are rejected, we know that Christ's own rejection, even on the cross, makes us precious in God's sight. Therefore we are no longer without God, but abide in God. Finally, the gift of grace through the power of the Spirit springs to life. We become not passive hearers only, but doers, living out our calls to vocation in daily life.

35. Meaninglessness/Call

Shirley Who Thinks She Is Completely Boring

Consider St. Paul's call story and Karen's story of Shirley: "Shirley is convinced she is completely boring. She actually does a lot to help her elderly neighbors each day, after reading a devotional and from her self-help books. Shirley has a sense of duty about caring for others. A few years back her congregation was 'boiling in controversy' and on the verge of splitting. Shortly thereafter Shirley's mother and father died, and then Shirley had a bout with cancer. It was then that she developed a sense that her life had lost all meaning.

"In the midst of this sense of meaninglessness, Shirley received a prayer shawl from the congregation and tangibly felt the love of a caring God. A knitter herself, gradually she felt called to start a prayer shawl ministry. 'Now this ministry is thriving,' she said, adding, 'we are knitting the congregation back together after the controversy.' The body of Christ image in Eph 4, particularly verse 16, 'the whole body, joined and knit together,' could have been of great help to Shirley; however, Shirley verbalizes what she is doing mainly through the language of her self-help books. When told that in all she does Shirley is proclaiming the good news of God calling us forth from the depths—or shallows—of meaninglessness, she said she had never thought of that.

Shirley has experienced Christ's call to discipleship and is ministering among her neighbors daily. However, she sees her work not as call but as duty. That is not to say she does it without joy, but she continues to measure herself against others who she seems to feel have more significant lives than she. As 'boring' as she may think she is, Shirley's ministry radiates throughout an entire Christian community, more than she realizes.[1]

In a twenty-first-century world there is a hunger for meaning and for an opportunity to make a difference. It is ironic that in the midst of our overly busy lives we may find ourselves trying to stave off boredom. (I'm speaking here from the context I know best, the global North.) With too many possibilities, we don't know what to do. When we simply do not want to be called on for one more thing, we still long for a call out of meaninglessness. All of this, too, is a part of the human predicament.

---

1. Einar Billing, *Our Calling* (Rock Island, IL: Augustana, 1958). Billing wrote, "Calling is and remains an everyday word, with a splendor of holy day about it, but its holy day splendor would disappear the moment it ceased to be a rather prosaic everyday word." "Calling" means Christians being called by grace to faith. "When it began to dawn on Luther that just as certainly as the call to [life with God] lifts us infinitely above everything that our everyday duties by themselves could give us, just that certainly the call does not take us away from these duties, but more deeply into them, then work became calling . . . call is primarily gift, and only in second or third place a duty" (5–8).

What does meaninglessness look like? It may appear as boredom. Or it may look like the opposite of boredom—a busy but empty life. Some people may lead positive, meaningful daily lives but not realize that others value their contributions. Others may be following pathways of destruction, or chasing after meaningless, even harmful, goals, or placing their trust in untrustworthy gods. Some may live with ongoing depression and the daily temptation to simply give up. They may see a reality in which all has become meaningless.

The gospel word needs to fit each person's particular situation. Call is not merely the result of salvation; it is the embodiment of salvation. In the midst of all that would keep us turned away from God and from one another—in this case, mired in a sense of meaninglessness—we are called forth, turned around, sent out toward new lives full of new meaning. The gospel call includes speaking and living the faith for others.

Paul's Call

In Gal 1:13–24 Paul gives his personal call story. (The account is fully detailed in Acts 8 and 9.) Here in the Epistle he says, "You have heard, no doubt, of my earlier life in Judaism." Formerly called Saul, Paul's life had been full of intentional meaning, as he himself says: "I was violently persecuting the church of God and was trying to destroy it." Furthermore, such zeal brought him advancement in his career "beyond many among my people of the same age" (v. 14).

When he was most centered on persecution, Paul recounts, God called him through grace and revealed God's Son, Jesus Christ, "so that I might proclaim him among the Gentiles" (v. 16). Paul's call was distinctly from God, and it was contrary to not only reason but also to his former best interests. Paul's call came in the midst of his following pathways devoted to destroying the Christian community. Of Paul it was then said, "The one who formerly was persecuting us is now proclaiming the faith he once tried to destroy" (v. 23). Many of the Pauline Epistles begin with Paul clearly stating the basis of his ministry—for example, 1 Cor 1:1, "Paul, called to be an apostle of Christ Jesus by the will of God . . ."

At first glance one would see few parallels between Shirley's and Paul's lives. Shirley considered herself completely boring. Paul was proud of his early career successes and his making a name for himself in trying to destroy the young church. The purpose of this book is not to draw quick parallels between one time in the church's history and another. However, church destruction permeates both stories. As Shirley put it, her congregation was "boiling in controversy."

At a deep level, members of Christ's church together are called to one calling, whatever our call stories. Sometimes we are turned around in our tracks; other times we are called simply in the midst of what we are already doing. Paul saw a bright light and was turned around. Shirley was dutifully caring for her elderly neighbors. Then her mother and father died and she herself was struggling with cancer. She received a prayer shawl from the congregation, then used her own gifts as a knitter (I doubt that Paul was a knitter!) and started a prayer shawl ministry.

In 1 Thess 1:4–5 we see that the entire church is called. God "has chosen you, because our message of the gospel came to you not in word only, but also in power and in the Holy Spirit and with full conviction . . ." Paul wrote to the church in Corinth, "to those who are sanctified in Christ Jesus, called to be saints, together with all those who in every place call on the name of our Lord Jesus Christ, both their Lord and ours" (1 Cor 1:2). Call has a double meaning in that verse; those who call on Christ are called to be saints—together. One is called to Christ, and that call cannot be separated from the call to discipleship. In 2 Thess 2:13 we read that the people are called to give thanks because "God chose you . . . for salvation through sanctification by the Spirit and through belief in the truth." Their lives are no longer meaningless; they are called (v. 14) through the "proclamation of the good news" in order to "obtain the glory of our Lord Jesus Christ."

In each case the letters to the churches begin by giving thanks to God, remembering their "work of faith and labor of love and steadfastness of hope in our Lord Jesus Christ" (1 Thess 1:3). Likewise, 2 Thessalonians begins with thanksgiving, "because your faith is growing abundantly, and the love of every one of you for one another is increasing" (1:3). Are these simply flattering words? There certainly is no shortage of criticism later in the Letters. No, this is not flattery; rather, the "grace to you and peace" in the greetings, in the name of their God and Savior Jesus Christ, is consistent and sure and grounding. The people who were without meaning, without call, are now called.

These churches are called for mission and ministry. In 1 Timothy we read of Timothy being urged to instruct the young Christians and their leaders that they are called to "pursue righteousness, godliness, faith, love, endurance, gentleness" and "take hold of the eternal life, to which you were called and for which you made the good confession in the presence of many witnesses" (6:11–12). There may be struggles, even falling back, as Paul writes to the Galatians: "I am astonished that you are so quickly deserting the one who called you in the grace of Christ and are turning to a different gospel—not that there is another gospel" (1:6–7). In Ephesians Paul begs the early Christians to "lead a life worthy of the calling" to which they had been called, "with all humility and gentleness, with patience, bearing with one another in love, making every effort to maintain the unity of the Spirit in the bond of peace" (4:1–3). "You were called to the one hope of your calling, one Lord, one faith, one baptism . . ." (v. 4). This same hope in Jesus Christ is both source and content of the call (Eph 1:18). It is God who calls through the proclamation of the good news, who makes Christians "worthy" of their call and who will "fulfill . . . every good resolve and work of faith" (2 Thess 1:11). This calling is for a new life, now and eternally, and the result is plural, new life together.

This new life may bring one suffering and shame; there is no mention of reward or prosperity on this earth. We are not called from poverty to riches, nor from illness to health, nor from obscurity to renown, but out of meaninglessness to new life. We are invited to share in the burdens of life—our own and others'. In the second letter to Timothy, we hear, "Do not be ashamed, then, of the testimony about our Lord or of me his prisoner, but join with me in suffering for the gospel, relying on the power of God, who saved us and called us with a holy calling, not according to our works but according to God's own purpose and grace" (1:8–9). This call is directly connected to "our Savior Christ Jesus, who abolished death and brought life and immortality to light through the gospel" (v. 10). This is a holy calling. After the call to grace, and closely associated with it, comes an appointment as "a herald and an apostle and a teacher" (v. 11). We need to be careful to avoid the error of thinking that only those who go to a theological school to study for a professional ministerial position in the church are considered to have "call stories." Call is central to salvation; all Christians have been called by and to the gospel through the power of the Spirit.

- Do you know anyone like Shirley who, in seeing their lives as mean-ingless, may be missing the sense of call they already have? When might you see this tendency in yourself?

- Pursue the language of "knitting the congregation back together." What does that mean? How does God do that? How might we use that language in addressing issues of conflict in the faith community?

- What are the languages of "self-help" books? What are some of the basic beliefs underlying the advice found in such books? How can a congregational study group compare and contrast that language with the language and promises of Scripture?

36. Futility/Purpose

God is faithful, particularly when we may question our sense of purpose in our present situation. The Epistles are full of clarity on God's calling us, even when we are not clear. We also find futility in the Epistles: "You must no longer live as the Gentiles live, in the futility of their minds" (Eph 4:17). "Gentiles" here refers to those without faith. The image is combined with "darkness" and being "alienated from the life of God" (v. 18). First Peter puts it this way: "You know you were ransomed from the futile ways inherited from your ancestors" (1:18). So this human predicament is not just our imagination, or "having a bad day," but experiencing something real. The term *futility* is used by Paul in relation to the creation itself: "the creation was subjected to futility, not of its own will but by the will of the one who subjected it . . ." (Rom 8:20). Futility has a power over people, and even creation. Perhaps you have felt such futility. Perhaps someone you know has experienced futility, utter futility, the sense of having no way out, even to the point of suicide. At just such a time the only news that is good enough comes from God's own self. The God who created all things "in accordance with the eternal purpose that God has carried out in Christ Jesus our Lord, in whom we have access to God in boldness and confidence through faith in him" (Eph 3:11).

Reciting a quick Bible verse is not adequate. A practice that sometimes leaves people more in doubt and more empty is the oft-quoted verse, "We know that all things work together for good for those who love God, who are called according to God's purpose" (Rom 8:28). "Purpose" and "call" are both in that sentence, but when all things do not seem to be working together for good, how does someone hear that verse?

The scriptural images open up new possibilities for us to listen in the languages people are speaking as they describe the context of their human situation, and to walk with them. We also need to listen to the context of the passage we are reading. In this case we need to go back to Rom 8:26 and read through to the end of the chapter, seeing that the Spirit searches the heart and intercedes for us with sighs too deep for words, that the one who calls also restores us to right relationships with God and with each other ("justification"), that God is for us and therefore no one can be against us. The chapter ends with the powerful assurance that nothing, even questioning our purpose in life, can separate us from the love of God in Christ Jesus.

Remain with God

God calls people to faith in Jesus Christ and thereby into God's service. Paul in 1 Cor 7:17–24 uses some direct language that can be very inviting, but also confusing: "let each of you lead the life that the Lord has assigned, to which God called you" (v. 17). The point is that the call need not change everything about one's former condition or situation: "Circumcision is nothing, and uncircumcision is nothing; but obeying the commandments of God is everything. Let each of you remain in the condition in which you were called" (vv. 19–20).

The problem comes when some people use this passage to keep other people in oppressive conditions. We spiritualize "call" to make it all about heaven and not at all about our roles and relationships here on earth. People have used 1 Cor 7:21 through the centuries to justify not dealing with the injustices of slavery: "Were you a slave when called? Do not be concerned about it." Note that the passage does not say that we should not deal with human suffering, abuse, or slavery, but rather, "In whatever condition you were called, brothers and sisters, there remain with God" (v. 24).

- As people called to live out their purpose in the world, how might your congregation reach out to members of the congregation and walk with them?

- How might you listen to a person who feels a sense of futility, while refraining from offering a quick Bible passage response? Where, in their own words, might you begin?

- How in Christ does the Spirit turn futility into purpose for us as individuals and as communities of faith? How can we use our calls to work for justice for those in oppressive conditions?

Naomi: Searching for Purpose through Community

Megan writes of her appreciation for Naomi: "I have known Naomi for a long time and am continually surprised as I encounter her in new ways.

At sixty-one, she has unadorned, natural beauty. Her nervous smile suggests a kind, shy person. Yet, in a group of trusted friends, she displays an unparalleled wit. Her hands show she has worked hard. She works twelve miles from home in a grocery store in a small town (with only one main street, some would hardly call it a town). The store itself reminds me of the pretend grocery store we had set up in my kindergarten classroom. There are only a few aisles. The hardware store is attached to the grocery. This is an unassuming place, no illusions of grandeur or global importance. Yet, for this community, it is a lifeline.

"The owners of this store know they are in a poor community, so they barter with vendors and often take a loss on some items. Naomi would be the first to tell you this is just a job, but she would also add, 'It's good enough for me.' Where one might see futility, one can also see friendliness and a tangible interconnectedness.

"Naomi greets everyone by name and answers mundane questions with patience. With those who are frail she asks for their list and helps gather the items. She later entrusted me with their stories—generally stories of pain, loss, and struggle. No matter how busy, she never hesitates to carry bags out to the parking lot for anyone who doesn't refuse. She has words of sadness, but no words of judgment. She knows who feels trapped in a bad marriage. She knows who is worn out from caring for a loved one. She sees the life of this community.

"After a long day on her feet, lifting, hauling, and running, Naomi's body is tired. She goes home to care for her husband. He has had a series of heart problems that leaves him without strength or endurance. He has had a hard time adjusting to this declined condition, and he takes it out on her—never physically, but with words that could break a weaker person.

"Naomi is a woman of deep faith, but she struggles to see the church as a faithful place. From her perspective the church isn't a place for asking questions or thinking about faith, but just a place to meet socially, and she feels like an outsider there. So Naomi takes her questions of faith elsewhere. She started taking classes in Healing Touch Ministries. Now she is a practitioner in that group and is working toward earning certification in Aromatherapy. I went with her to one gathering and as they prayed, healed with touch, and mutually shared their struggles and hopes, I saw a powerful healing community at work.

"Naomi, of course, carries regrets and guilt, but these are not her primary struggles of faith. She is searching for purpose amid futility and a way to encounter God in daily life. I want to believe the community she finds in Healing Touch could also be found in her church. How do we create a place that is safe for this kind of authentic vulnerability?"

37. Uselessness/Gifts

In 1 Cor 1:4–9 we see God's faithful calling. The passage begins with Paul's giving thanks to God always because of the "grace of God that has been given you in Christ Jesus," a grace that transforms one from feeling useless to someone whose gifts are useful. The passage goes on, "for in every way you have been enriched in him, in speech and knowledge of every kind . . . so that you are not lacking in any spiritual gift as you wait for the revealing of our Lord Jesus Christ." "The free gift of God is eternal life in Christ Jesus our Lord" (Rom 6:22). "The gifts and the calling of God are irrevocable" (Rom 11:29). And, "Of this gospel I have become a servant according to the gift of God's grace that was given me . . ." (Eph 3:7). The context of each of these passages deserves greater study; however, what is clear is that one important image of grace in various places in the Epistles is "gift," the "surpassing grace of God" that God has given: "Thanks be to God for God's indescribable gift" (2 Cor 9:14–15).

Likewise, the three great body of Christ passages all connect Christians to one another by emphasizing that all of the parts are necessary. None is useless. We are gifts to one another, not in useless or "some greater than others" ways; all are useful, and all directly connected to Christ and to one another.[2] First Corinthians 12:12: "For just as the body is one and has many members, and all the members of the body, though many, are one body, so it is with Christ." Later we see the gifts named: apostles, prophets, teachers, deeds of power, gifts of healing, forms of assistance, forms of leadership, various kinds of tongues (v. 28). Just as not all have the same gifts, not all have the same roles, but all are useful and important in the body. Paul concludes by saying, "But strive for the greater gifts. And I will show you a still more excellent way" (v. 31). The gifts are varied, and the greater gift is love, which Paul describes in chapter 13 of 1 Corinthians.

In the Eph 4:1–16 body of Christ passage, we also are called to bear with one another in love. "Each of us was given grace according to the

2. In chapter 4 the image of Division/Unity explores these same three body of Christ passages from the standpoint of the human predicament as being divided and grace as being united in Christ.

measure of Christ's gift" (v. 7). Not the measure of our own gifts, but the grace of Christ's gift. The varieties of gifts are an integral part of grace: apostles, prophets, evangelists, pastors, and teachers (v. 11). Again, it should be emphasized that the list is open and the gifts are not ranked. The gifts of grace are for the purpose of equipping the saints to use their own gifts and therefore to build up the body of Christ (v. 12).

Likewise, in the third body of Christ passage, Rom 12, we are called to let "love be genuine" (v. 9) and "not to think of yourself more highly than you ought to think" (v. 3). Here grace is used in a slightly different way; "gifts differ according to the grace given to us" (v. 6), but still it is God's grace. One does not measure the amount of grace nor the usefulness of the gifts (which would be counter to verse 3 above). Rather, we hear that all should use the gifts they have: "prophecy, in proportion to faith; ministry, in ministering; the teacher, in teaching; the exhorter, in exhortation; the giver, in generosity; the leader, in diligence; the compassionate, in cheerfulness" (vv. 6–8). None is useless. All gifts are part of the grace of God in Christ Jesus.

The Epistles themselves make no strong case for certain offices in the church, although we do see the laying on of hands: "Do not neglect the gift that is in you, which was given to you through the prophecy with the laying on of hands by the council of elders" (1 Tim 4:14). Also, "For this reason I remind you to rekindle the gift of God that is within you through the laying on of my hands; for God did not give us a spirit of cowardice, but rather a spirit of power and of love and of self-discipline" (2 Tim 1:6–7). In both of these texts, although there is an external action by members of the faith community (people are called forth), the gifts are within, acts of the grace of God. And although there are descriptions of what good leaders are to be like, we hear of no useless people. There is no issue of class. One needs to include the slave Onesimus, for example; the case Paul made for returning Onesimus to Philemon is that "formerly he was useless to you, but now he is indeed useful both to you and to me" (Phlm 11). Commentaries have assumed that that meant he was not a good slave—but one could perhaps also make the case that being useful is a gift closely associated with new life in Christ.

The image of grace as gift includes all; we are called to use these gifts and to share the gift of the grace of God. "Like good stewards of the manifold grace of God, serve one another with whatever gift each of you has received. Whoever speaks must do so as one speaking the very words of God;

whoever serves must do so with the strength that God supplies, so that God may be glorified in all things through Jesus Christ" (1 Pet 4:10–11).

Mike the Maintenance Man

After walking and talking with Mike, Kyle shares this story: "I walked with Mike, a man in his mid-fifties, during his shift as a maintenance employee. I met up with Mike and his coworkers at about 7 a.m. He spends his time most days keeping the mechanical systems of the building in order, working on the grounds around the building, and doing odd jobs. Once in a while he is asked to go out and pick up supplies, such as mopheads, cleaners, and even tires. Mike has been at this job longer than anyone else except for the maintenance supervisor, so most of the part-time workers come to him for instruction or advice.

"Mike calls upon his years of experience in this field when a problem arises. If an issue requires more than technical skill, however, he calls upon values that are informed by his lifelong faith. He seems to take most of what the Roman Catholic Church teaches as what should be believed. As we drove around in the work truck, Mike had the radio tuned to well-known conservative talk show personalities.

"Mike and his coworkers speak the language of maintenance workers. Their experiences at work together revolve around fixing, building, and upkeep. As we sat at the main table in the maintenance shop there was some small talk about the weather and such. Mike's main task for the day was to replace some special filters in the ventilation system of the building. This required maneuvering into a small attic-type crawl space. Here Mike explained to me what the specific machine did and why it was important the filters were changed. When the air hit a certain rotating circle of perforated metal, the temperature of the air that came from outside the building was transferred to the air coming into the building. That way the fresh air from the outside required less energy to get to the temperature that was desired inside. The filters that needed replacing stopped the part of the machine that transferred the air temperature from getting clogged with the dust and other particles in the air.

"This started us on the topic of making the building more 'green.' As Mike and I walked back to the maintenance shop, he told me about many of the other things the company was doing to care for the environment. They had started using lower wattage and fewer light bulbs in their ceiling fixtures, recycling, and sending e-mails instead of printing memos. I asked Mike what he thought of all of that, and he said it was a good idea to take care of the planet. He had recently had a third grandchild, and he talked a little bit about making sure the world was around when his grandchildren grew up. I got the feeling that he wasn't the most ecologically minded person I'd ever met but that he recognized the importance of caring for the planet.

"Mike and I were able to have some good conversation. He said he didn't consider what he does in life a ministry; it is maintenance. I suggested that making sure the air is clean so people don't get sick and keeping the vehicles in good condition could be and are ways of helping people. He still seemed almost uncomfortable with the idea that he ministers to people when he does this kind of work, perhaps because he has heard more often than not that pastors and priests do ministry."

(As I place this story in this chapter I hear out my window—and then stand up to see—a garbage truck, a recycling truck, and a school bus all going by at the same time. All bright yellow. All driven by *real* people, faithful in doing their jobs well. Our neighbor, Bob, has a conversation with one of the drivers. A *real* conversation, in the midst of daily life, a gift of grace among all these very useful people.)

38. Of No Value/Bought

In the twenty-first century, a person's *value* is of great concern. Does one have value? And in whose eyes? Everything from supermarket coupons to stock market shares are spoken of in terms of how much they are worth, or for how long they can be redeemed or cashed in. Often people feel like commodities. Much of the first part of Romans convicts the readers of being of no value, of being sinners and worthless—as when Paul, quoting Ps 14, says, "All have turned aside, together they have become worthless" (3:12). The nature of the human predicament then and now is that people most often feel that worthlessness. Even those with economic security may feel they are of little or no value and therefore need to keep proving themselves. Do you know people like that? Is that not our own reality at times?

In 1 Cor 6:20 we have the familiar words, "For you were bought with a price; therefore glorify God in your body." Also, "You are bought with a price; do not become slaves of human masters" (1 Cor 7:23). For people for whom the image of being of no value describes their human predicament, the image of grace as being bought may be a place to start.

Similarly, one could look at the images of the word "redeem," such as Jesus "gave himself for us that he might redeem us from all iniquity and purify for himself a people of his own who are zealous for good deeds" (Titus 2:14). Here Christ "gave" rather than bought. But "redeem" has this connotation. This redemption is for the purpose of people's lives being changed for zeal for good deeds—surely the opposite of having no value. In 1 Timothy we have the word "ransom": "For there is one God; there is also one mediator between God and humankind, Christ Jesus, himself human who gave himself a ransom for all . . ." (2:5–6).

- Do you or someone you know struggle with feeling as if you are of no value? What is it like to live in a world where one's worth is always being measured?

- Think about these words: "bought," "gave," "redeem," "ransom." How do they speak to you about what Christ has done for you on the cross?

39. Earned Worth/Salvation

When something has no value or has to be redeemed or bought, we might consider it salvaged. It now has purpose. "Salvation" is a central word in Christianity, but we rarely view it is this way. We have been salvaged, saved from danger or destruction, delivered from sin and death through Jesus Christ. A core verse for this image is Eph 2:8, "For by grace you have been saved through faith, and this is not your own doing; it is the gift of God . . ." Also significant: "God, who is rich in mercy, out of the great love with which he loved us . . . made us alive together with Christ—by grace you have been saved" (Eph 2:4–5).[3] In 2 Cor 6:2 we read, "Now is the acceptable time; see, now is the day of salvation!" Ephesians 1:13 has "the word of truth, the gospel of your salvation."

Salvation is power. Paul writes, "For I am not ashamed of the gospel; it is the power of God for salvation to everyone who has faith, to the Jew first and also to the Greek" (Rom 1:16). This salvation in Christ Jesus comes to us through faith (v. 17). "For God has destined us not for wrath but

3. "Salvation" by grace is the subject of this entire book. (Soteriology is the theology of salvation.) In Image 39 we also use Earned Worth/Salvation as one specific image in the Epistles. One could also trace the many uses of the words "save" and "saved" in the Epistles.

for obtaining salvation through our Lord Jesus Christ" (1 Thess 5:9). We are then to take the "helmet of salvation" (Eph 6:17). Jesus is the "source of eternal salvation" through his obedience and suffering (Heb 5:8–9) and therefore the "pioneer" of salvation. Salvation is both sure and dynamic at the same time.

Titus 2:11: "For the grace of God has appeared, bringing salvation to all." It is interesting that salvation "appears." Salvation is "training us to renounce" things that one could describe as disobedience: impiety, worldly passions, etc. (v. 12). In 1 Tim 4:10 "we have our hope set on the living God, who is the Savior of all people, especially of those who believe." This could lead us to ask questions about the intended recipients of salvation . . . beyond believers.

In Phil 1:28 the Christians are in no way to be intimidated by opponents because "this is evidence of their destruction, but of your salvation." Philippians 2:12 is that thought-provoking verse, "Work out your own salvation with fear and trembling." This does not mean that by our works we earn our worth, but rather that we grow in the gift of salvation already ours through Jesus Christ. "Like newborn infants, long for the pure, spiritual milk, so that by it you grow into salvation—if indeed you have tasted that the Lord is good" (1 Pet 2:2). Salvation was promised; it is now and is to come in the last days, according to 1 Pet 1:3–11: "Concerning this salvation, the prophets who prophesied of the grace that was to be yours . . ." (v.10); "for you are receiving the outcome of your faith, the salvation of your souls" (v. 9); and by God's great mercy we "are being protected by the power of God through faith for a salvation ready to be revealed in the last time" (v. 5). And this salvation is not just personal. It is always communal: "Beloved, while eagerly preparing to write to you about the salvation we share . . ." (Jude 3).

Pam: "Will God Stop Loving Me?"

After accompanying Pam, Julie tells this story: "Many times Pam would tell me, 'I need to work harder, and do better, so God will not stop loving me. I do not want to lose my salvation. If other people can walk away from me, then so will God.' We journeyed together through Scripture this past month; she seemed anxious to talk. Now she was hearing God's salvation was a free gift, not something she had to earn. 'How can that be? I spent my whole life earning things, trying to measure up in order to deserve them, only to lose much of what I thought was mine and could never lose.' Pam had occasionally flipped through a pew Bible, but now, together, we read Eph 2:8, 'For by grace you have been saved through faith, and this is not your own doing; it is the gift of God.' We emphasized the words 'grace' and 'gift.' Pam replied, 'Is this what you and Pastor mean when you preach about God's love?'"

- Have you heard the words of Scripture but never really understood salvation as grace? In what ways can we study the Bible together so that Scripture permeates our daily lives?

- How is salvation already "accomplished" and at the same time something yet to come?

40. Disobedience/Obedience

This image is so often assumed to be the central issue of the Christian faith, even though it is not a major image in terms of frequency of use in the Epistles. Of course it is important, because human beings are disobedient to God. Ephesians 2:2 speaks of people "following the ruler of the power of the air, the spirit that is now at work among those who are disobedient."

Among those who have left the church or who have never entered one, the reason often given is because they feel they are being judged permanently for some particular instance of disobedience in their lives. Actually, all of us are disobedient in God's eyes: "For God has imprisoned all in disobedience so that God may be merciful to all" (Rom 11:32). Romans 5:19 reads, "For just as by the one man's disobedience the many were made sinners, so by the one man's obedience the many will be made righteous."

Doing good out of a sense of duty or "obedience" is to live still under the law. In this way we continue to try to justify ourselves in front of others and before God. We hear every day wonderful stories of people doing kind, generous, even amazingly helpful things, but too often we hear the added phrase, "It makes me feel so good." Doing good out of a sense of duty or even in an attempt to obey only turns in on oneself. Christ alone became obedient, and through his obedience, as a gift, we have become obedient. Grace. Even our obedience is transformed. (Paul links "obedience" with welcoming hospitality in 2 Cor 7: 15.) Out of grace, we are called not to do things so that we will feel good, but to vocations of generosity and kindness that are open-ended and grace-filled.

- Do you know people who are staying away from the church for fear of being judged? How can you meet them where they are and share grace as did Christ who became obedient for us?

- None of us has pure motivations; however, how does the gift of grace free us for vocations of generosity?

41. Rejected/Precious

Some people may consider themselves beyond God's reach or care. Perhaps even more despairing is to think oneself as rejected by God, rejected by human beings, rejected by everyone. We see this image of rejection in 1 Peter. For the one who has experienced rejection the good news is that Christ himself was rejected, throughout his lifetime and, most tellingly, on the cross. "For it stands in scripture: 'See, I am laying in Zion a stone, a cornerstone chosen and precious; and whoever believes in him will not be put to shame'" (1 Pet 2:6).[4] "The stone that the builder rejected has become the very head of the corner" (1 Pet 2:7).[5]

Christ, the rejected one, has become the precious one, and we are invited to come to him. We are invited to no longer feel rejected, but to be included. For some it may be a totally new concept to think of themselves as valued and precious, as part of a holy priesthood. "Come to him, a living stone, though rejected by mortals yet chosen and precious in God's sight, and like living stones, let yourselves be built into a spiritual house, to be a holy priesthood, to offer spiritual sacrifices acceptable to God through Jesus Christ" (1 Pet 2:4–5).

- What does this image say to you when you reflect on those times when you have been rejected?

- What does this image say about the prominent place God calls the once rejected to take within the house of God, within the priesthood of all believers? How do we now reach out to those whom the world—and sometime the church—rejects?

4. Quoted from Is 28:16
5. Quoted from Ps 118:22

42. Without God/Abiding in God

God has created all humanity, so who can say that anyone is without God? And yet God being beyond our reach is not only a scriptural image but a very real feeling for many people. The Ephesians passages that provided the image of divisions between Christians of Gentile birth and those of Jewish birth also can be read in this image when we think of being "far off" as being "without God": "But now in Christ Jesus you who once were far off have been brought near by the blood of Christ. . . . So he came and proclaimed peace to you who were far off" (Eph 2:13, 17). And a chapter later, we read that "in Christ Jesus our Lord . . . we have access to God in boldness and confidence through faith in him" (3:12). This is so that "Christ may dwell in your hearts through faith," and "so that you may be filled with all the fullness of God" (3:17, 19). This is the good news.

Through Christ we abide in God and the Spirit abides in us: "You are in the Spirit, since the Spirit of God dwells in you" (Rom 8:9). The God who raised Christ from the dead gives life to our mortal bodies through God's Spirit "that dwells in you" (Rom 8:11).

Not surprisingly, the Letters of John often use the image of abiding in God: "Whoever says, 'I abide in him,' ought to walk just as he walked" (1 John 2:6); "If what you heard from the beginning abides in you, then you will abide in the Son and in the Father. And this is what he has promised us, eternal life" (1 John 2:24–25); "We know that he abides in us, by the Spirit that he has given us" (1 John 3:24); "By this we know that we abide in him and he in us, because he has given us of his Spirit. . . . God abides in those who confess that Jesus is the Son of God, and they abide in God" (1 John 4:13, 15); and the culminating, familiar verse, "God is love, and those who abide in love abide in God, and God abides in them" (1 John 4:16).

There is also a challenge in these Johannine verses: How does God's love abide in anyone who has the world's goods and who sees a brother or sister in need but refuses help? Others may be without the necessities of life. To have God's love abide in us is also a communal, grace-filled call to vocation.

- The God who is the Creator of the universe also abides within us, the created ones. How can that be? What does that mean for our daily existence? Our daily ministry?

- Have you felt at times that God is a far-distant God? Out of reach? Do you feel that way even now? To whom can you go to be reassured that you are not, never have been, and never will be without God?

The Silver Screen Canteen

Nate witnesses Molly and Terry's vocation: "I have spent many hours at the Silver Screen Canteen, sipping a house brew and noshing on cheesecake while preparing for sermons or confirmation classes. This time when I arrived the lobby was largely deserted for my conversation with Molly, co-owner with her husband, Terry, who was out sick that day. The quiet atmosphere was occasionally punctuated by a customer in need of a quick latte on his way to work. The UPS delivery man came in and a theater patron from the night before dropped by, hoping to reclaim a glove she believed she had left at the theater.

"Molly and Terry felt a call to this kind of work years ago when they worked at a café downtown, next to a pottery shop, an art studio, and a yoga studio. They felt their work was to serve people without consistent incomes, health care, or even transportation. Because of this experience Molly and Terry finally followed their dream and opened the Silver Screen Canteen. Profit margins are very thin. The West End customers tend to be less financially desperate, but those who drop in struggle with loneliness, even rejection. They wrestle with guilt over bad choices they have made in the past. Molly sees her vocation as one in which she can offer blessing, acceptance, and even some form of connectedness. She winced when I mentioned the word 'ministry' because she said it made her think of the kind of person who gives out unhelpful advice, someone who might make moral judgments. 'That's just my role.' Then she added, 'I guess what I do *is* ministry, but just not in those ways.'

"After I had been at the theater for about an hour, 'Mary' came in to speak with Molly. Molly asked me if she could be excused for a few minutes. Forty-five minutes later Molly came back and apologized for taking so long; she had been speaking with 'Mary' as a Stephen Minister. I was not surprised to hear that, even though, of course, the conversation with 'Mary' was confidential. Terry and Molly attend a local Lutheran church that trains lay people to serve as Stephen Ministers, linking them with people going through difficult times in their lives, such as grief. While Stephen Ministers often meet in people's homes, this setting worked just fine.

"In everything they do, Molly and Terry, in the setting of this entertainment center, entertain people with generous hospitality. They abide in Christ and people find in them a place to abide. They are not only hearers but doers of the Word."

43. Only Hearers/Doers

It is ironic that we human beings, in our sinful condition, as part of our human predicament, have the propensity both to consider our lives useless, meaningless, and futile and to try to prove and justify ourselves before God and other people by the very good works that we do. How can we have it both ways? The latter may be a sign of the inadequacy of the former. We may try so hard to prove ourselves *because* we consider ourselves inadequate and meaningless in the face of God.

Paul, particularly in the first part of Romans, spends considerable time telling his readers that they are not righteous before God. "For it is not the hearers of the law who are righteous in God's sight, but the doers of the law who will be justified" (2:13). And who can keep the entire law? Who is ever good enough? Who can ever do enough? That is the problem. At best we can only be hearers of God's will for us.

There are other places in the Epistles where the futility of trying to be justified by the law is made clear. In Galatians Paul asks, "Did you receive the Spirit by doing the works of the law or by believing what you heard? . . . Well then, does God supply you with the Spirit and work miracles among you by your doing the works of the law, or by your believing what you heard?" (3:2, 5). Grace is made clear: "I do not nullify the grace of God; for if justification comes through the law, then Christ died for nothing" (2:21).

The gift of grace that makes all the difference in daily life is that God *does* supply us with the Spirit, not to justify ourselves, but through the freedom of faith. God even works miracles through believers for the sake of the hurting neighbor and for the healing of the world. Our work is no longer futile; our lives, and we ourselves, are no longer useless. We have not been rejected. We are not without God or of no value, but we have been bought, redeemed, and saved for a purpose—to be doers of the Word: "But be doers of the word, and not merely hearers who deceive themselves. For if any are hearers of the word and not doers, they are like those who look at themselves in a mirror; for they look at themselves and, on going away, immediately forget what they were like. But those who look into the perfect law, the law of liberty, and persevere, being not hearers who forget but do-ers who act—they will be blessed in their doing" (Jas 1:22–25).

James, often misquoted or dismissed, goes on: "What good is it, my brothers and sisters, if you say you have faith but do not have works? Can faith save you? If a brother or sister is naked and lacks daily food, and one of you says to them, 'Go in peace; keep warm and eat your fill,' and yet you do not supply their bodily needs, what is the good of that? So faith by itself, if it has not works, is dead. But someone will say, 'You have faith and I have works.' Show me your faith apart from your works, and I by my works will show you my faith" (Jas 2:14–18).

- How have things been turned completely around, from living in meaninglessness to "by God's grace in Jesus Christ" being given a variety of gifts to care for those in need?

- As a faith community, how can we meet people where they are in their feelings of being without value, without God, and through our actions show them that they are called, precious, and that God abides in them, so that they may become actors in God's purposeful mission and ministry in their daily lives?

Brian at the Bookstore

Chad tells the following story of his walk with Brian: "I walked with Brian, who works at a bookstore. His shift on this particular day started at 10:00 a.m. Brian primarily was at the checkout register. While a line of customers soon grew, he took time to give each customer his undivided attention. He stepped away from the register if a customer had a particular question on a book.

"As I watched Brian on the store floor I continued to see his sincerity in helping customers. He says he enjoys working the floor more than working the register and is knowledgeable about the products. This is something the customers greatly appreciate. After his shift ended, I sat down with him to learn about his background working in retail for the past seven years, along with the ups and the downs of his position.

"One of the greatest joys Brian has in working at the bookstore is the opportunity to help people find books that may in fact be helpful in their lives. He takes the time to be with them until they have exactly what they are looking for. He said there have been people who are struggling to understand autism because a family member or a friend has autism.

"A downside to working at the bookstore is the long shifts due to the store being open seven days a week. Sometimes he can't attend church. Brian also finds it hard when the occasional customer gets frustrated and begins yelling at him, or throwing things at him (which happened during a Black Friday shift). However, he said he tries to not let those moments hold him back from helping others.

"Along with observing and talking with Brian, I observed the variety of customers who came through the store, from the youth to the grandparents. Their reasons for shopping were no doubt varied as well. Our society holds varying myths about retail. It seems people thrive on shopping, particularly around the time of my visit, which was just after the major Black Friday event. However, there tends to also be negative connotations about those who work in retail. Many may wonder why you would want to work in retail when there are so many other 'better' jobs. It is a challenging position to be in, and yet, despite the challenges, I can tell Brian finds purpose in what he does.

"The day I walked with Brian was a calmer day at the store, and the emotions were ones of contentment, of laughter and enjoyment. This is not always the case. A bookstore can be a place that presents the human condition in a very open way. There are plenty of self-help books on how to structure one's business just right, on how to have the perfect recipe or the perfect body.

"On the other hand, a bookstore can also be a place of peace in which to rejuvenate oneself and be at peace. Reading creates an opportunity to be creative and to imagine a multitude of things. I believe that is why the store where Brian works is an excellent place for his vocation.

"With the many long hours people in retail put in to serve the public and the various times they might have to deal with angry customers, which might leave them feeling drained, discouraged, and wondering if there is any merit in what they do, Brian's ability to connect with customers provides a ministry beyond people's initial purchase. There is meaning to his daily vocation."

CHAPTER 6

Beyond Suffering toward Hope

Into the relentless situation of suffering, hostility, and persecution in our world enters the Christ who endured it all; in Jesus is hope. All of the images in this chapter touch on suffering. "Cast all your anxiety on God, because God cares for you" (1 Pet 5:7). Anxiety ranks high in all settings of daily life. And how does one believe in God the protector when one's life experience tells a different story?

Judgment belongs to God. Yet so often people suffer unjustly because of the judgmental attitudes and actions of others. Mercy rests in the unconditional love of God. But what if we do not experience that love? Grace as God's love is directly connected to God's love flowing through God's beloved in their ministries in daily life. Atonement comes through Christ's offering himself as a sacrifice; this is communal grace. Being cleansed is the work of the Spirit in Jesus Christ, the work of justification and sanctification.

Shame is a deeply rooted human emotion. The strong Word of grace meets people at that place of the shamed self. The image of Labor/Rest speaks to us when we think we are saved by our own labor or when work becomes burdensome under unjust systems of economic inequality. Rest is gift and grace. For individuals stuck in inertia and congregations mired in apathy, "standing" and "walking" can be important images offering purpose, direction, and hope.

44. Persecution, Hostility, Suffering/ Patience, Consolation, Joy

People everywhere, in all times, have faced all degrees of hostility and persecution, from oppression under unjust systems, prejudice, bullying, and sexual violence to death itself. Stop for a moment and picture the human predicament in its various forms. Suffering enters every life at some point. One person's suffering cannot be ranked as greater or less than another's. Each one's suffering is sad, often tragic. Christ, who endured our suffering, brings patience and consolation, even joy.

In 1 Thess 1:6 Paul said that "in spite of persecution you received the word with joy inspired by the Holy Spirit . . ." Persecution and suffering connect us (1 Thess 2:14). No matter the difference in severity or cause, "persecution" and "suffering" are associated with communal pain. The result, being connected to Christ's unjust suffering, produces courage (1 Thess 2:2). Suffering, persecution, and mistreatment can be taken to the cross.

What are the causes of suffering? People even today often interpret suffering as God's punishment, when in the Epistles it is most often connected with Christ's own suffering. This suffering is "for the sake of the gospel" (2 Tim 1:8). Through suffering we are connected to Christ (1 Pet 4:1). We are told to not be surprised by the amount of suffering in the world, but to "rejoice insofar as you are sharing Christ's sufferings" (1 Pet 4:13). In the midst of the questions is the reality that "Jesus Christ, raised from the dead . . . is my gospel, for which I suffer hardship," as the writer of 2 Tim 2:8–9 says. "Therefore I endure everything for the sake of the elect, so that they may also obtain the salvation that is in Christ Jesus, with eternal glory. The saying is sure: If we have died with him, we will also live with him; if we endure, we will also reign with him . . ." (vv. 10–12). The strength we need "to endure everything with patience" comes "from his glorious power"; this strength is accompanied by joy (Col 1:11).

In Philippians Paul goes further: "For God has graciously granted you the privilege not only of believing in Christ, but of suffering for him as well—since you are having the same struggle that you saw I had and now hear that I still have" (1:29–30). We dare not presume to tell people that their suffering is a privilege for them. However, being connected with Christ's suffering means being part of the suffering of all humanity.

God is a God of consolation who "consoles us in our affliction, so that we may be able to console those who are in any affliction with the consolation with which we ourselves are consoled by God" (2 Cor 1:4). We are joined with Christ in affliction; grace empowers us to console others. This consolation is not just an add-on to being saved but is central to grace itself. The passage goes on, "For just as the sufferings of Christ are abundant for us, so also our consolation is abundant through Christ. . . . Our hope for you is unshaken; for we know that as you share in our sufferings, so also you share in our consolation" (vv. 5, 7).

This same image is in 2 Cor 7:6 and 9. God "consoles the downcast" by the arrival of Titus, and likewise he was consoled "about you." Suffering is part of the human predicament in every age. In Christ's suffering we experience the consolation of God.

Trish: Heartbreak and Consolation

Sara observes and listens with care to Trish, then tells this story: "Trish supervises the child and protective services and children's mental health units at the county department of human services where she lives. She has worked in the field of social work for twenty-five years. Trish finds her work very fulfilling, although at times the situations she encounters can be heartbreaking. Her primary work is to provide counsel, advice, and support to her staff. She steps in to work on cases as need arises for high-profile or particularly urgent cases. She also acts as liaison between the county and local police and occasionally attends court hearings.

"Recently a mother took her two young children from the foster care home where they had been placed and absconded with them. Trish worked closely with detectives and all breathed a sigh of relief when the mother finally agreed, after hiding out with the grandmother, to turn herself in and safely return the children.

"Each day Trish is faced acutely with the realities of the human predicament. She sees children abused and neglected, families torn apart by drug and alcohol problems. These struggles are exacerbated by job loss and financial stress.

"But even in the midst of it all there is an abundance of grace. Children are not simply grabbed from their homes and placed in foster care; parents do not just lose their parental rights. Parents are given the chance to make amends, to serve time if it is required, to find steady employment, to get clean, to be better. Many social workers have an innate drive to work with parents and children to correct problems, bring healing, and restore wholeness.

"The families with whom Trish works are not strangers to persecution, hostility, and suffering. But Trish and her staff help these families find consolation, joy, and hope and offer them no small amount of patience as they work together. Likewise, Trish and her staff, too, are not strangers to persecution, hostility, and suffering in the form of continued cuts in funding from the state. There is never a good time for cuts to come, but in the past few years, they have come when there has been a significant increase in people seeking help from the department of human services at the county level. That means the agency is trying to do more with fewer resources. The meetings to figure out how to continue to provide services are draining and frustrating. The staff practice patience while they wait and hope for funding to return. Trish believes God is at work in all social workers who practice grace and mercy and work with and for those who have no voice."

Wounds Remain but Grace Continues

"By his wounds you have been healed" (1 Pet 2:24). This is true and yet wounds remain. "Beloved, I pray that all may go well with you and that you may be in good health, just as it is well with your soul" (3 John 2). And yet, so often things are not that way. Our hope—steadfastness—in the resurrection is sure, which is quite different than "hoping" things turn out okay. Ministering in daily life while working on behalf of the persecuted will bring resistance, although differently in each century: "Indeed, all who want to live a godly life in Christ Jesus will be persecuted" (2 Tim 3:12).

Living in grace calls for enduring patience, and the gift of Christ is deep consolation and joy beyond mere happiness. So we read in Hebrews, "let us run with perseverance the race that is set before us, looking to Jesus the pioneer and perfecter of our faith, who for the sake of the joy that was set before him endured the cross. . . . Consider him who endured such hostility against himself from sinners, so that you may not grow weary or lose heart" (12:1–3).

First Peter 1:6, 8–9: "In this you rejoice, even if now for a little while you have had to suffer various trials. . . . Although you have not seen him, you love him; and even though you do not see him now, you believe in him and rejoice with an indescribable and glorious joy, for you are receiving the outcome of your faith, the salvation of your souls." First Peter chapters 2 and 3 dwell on Christ's suffering; in chapter 2 Peter reminds his readers that when Christ was abused he did not return the abuse, and urges them to endure suffering and abuse even when they have done no wrong (vv. 19–25). We realize, after many centuries, how these verses have been misused to justify injustice and to keep the oppressed and the abused under the power of their abusers. Let us not be co-opted into participating in perpetuating abuse. We are called through Christ's resurrection to engage in liberating, healing ministries.

"Therefore, let those suffering in accordance with God's will entrust themselves to a faithful Creator, while continuing to do good" (1 Pet 4:19). And finally, "After you have suffered for a little while, the God of all grace, who has called you to God's eternal glory in Christ, will himself restore, support, strengthen, and establish you" (1 Pet 5:10).

Living in the grace of God intrinsically means a call to endure suffering, not as duty but as gift and call to ministry in daily life: "As for you, always be sober, endure suffering, do the work of an evangelist, carry out your ministry fully" (2 Tim 4:5). And "endure anything rather than put an obstacle in the way of the gospel of Christ" (1 Cor 9:12). In Ephesians we read, "I pray therefore that you may not lose heart over my sufferings for you . . ." (3:13).

But just as surely as sufferings, persecutions, and hostility are part of living in the grace of God in Christ Jesus, so surely the good news is that God consoles, grants hope, and gives the strength to endure. Suffering, while often not removed, is transformed and often appears as hope. "For in hope we were saved. Now hope that is seen is not hope. For who hopes for what is seen? But if we hope for what we do not see, we wait for it with patience" (Rom 8:24–25). And a few verses later we are assured that "hardship, or distress, or persecution" (v. 35) will not separate us from the love of Christ. Therefore, we can "rejoice in hope, be patient in suffering, persevere in prayer" (Rom 12:12).

In the letters to the Corinthians we see this grace put into action: "When reviled, we bless; when persecuted, we endure; when slandered, we speak kindly" (1 Cor 4:12–13). The sufferings will continue, even to the point of being "utterly, unbearably crushed" and despairing "of life itself" (2 Cor 1:8), but, as we read in verse 5, more so will consolation continue: "For just as the sufferings of Christ are abundant for us, so also our consolation is abundant through Christ." (Read all of 2 Cor 1:3–7.) "Therefore I am content with weaknesses, insults, hardships, persecutions, and calamities for the sake of Christ . . ." (2 Cor 12:10). Finally we have the powerful words of 2 Cor 4:7–10: "We have this treasure in clay jars. . . . We are afflicted in every way, but not crushed; perplexed, but not driven to despair; persecuted, but not forsaken; struck down, but not destroyed; always carrying in the body the death of Jesus . . ."

- In what ways has suffering been part of your life? How and through whom have you been consoled? Has the suffering been removed? Has it worsened? Changed?

- In what ways have you experienced, or witnessed, or even participated in hostility and persecution? Where do you see it in the world today? How can Christ's own endurance of persecution and death transform personal and societal persecution and hostilities? How can you and your faith community become involved in such transformational ministries?

- What does "hope" mean to you? How can we be both patient and hopeful at the same time?

45. Anxiety/Care

The concluding chapter of 1 Peter begins with the words, "Now as an elder myself and a witness of the sufferings of Christ . . ." (5:1). And a few verses later: "And after you have suffered for a little while, the God of all grace who has called you to eternal glory in Christ, will restore, support strengthen and establish you" (1 Pet 5:10).

In between is the often quoted verse "Cast all your anxiety on God, because God cares for you" (1 Pet 5:7). In this twenty-first-century North American context, anxiety ranks high among daily sufferings in people from all walks of life. Anxiety may need to be treated medically and with counseling; multiple forms of anxiety and depression and deeper levels of mental illness touch so many families. Here we include anxiety also as an image of the human predicament and grace as care. In the midst of dealing with anxiety, we can cast it *all* upon God.

The good news may not be that anxiety or its cause will be removed or even alleviated, but that God cares. There is nothing so anxiety-producing that it is beyond the grace of God in Christ Jesus. In our ministry to people in their real lives the Gospel message they need to hear at that moment may not be "You are forgiven," or that "the Bible is true" but that surely, "God cares."

- Have you or someone dear to you ever suffered from anxiety or do you or they now? What does it feel like? How does it affect one's daily life? Relationships? Faith life?

- How does—or might—the good news that God knows and cares in the midst of any and all anxiety make a difference in daily life during the struggles?

Jack on the Tracks

Reed listens to Jack and relates his story: "'My biggest worry is that we're heading down the tracks at sixty miles per hour and there is a car stopped on a crossing ahead. We try to stop, but it takes too much time and we smash into the vehicle.' This quote from Jack, a railway conductor, is a harrowing one and a reminder of the anxiety of those who spend their days or nights running trains weighing thousands of tons and sometimes stretching for over a mile. Although railroad-related fatalities may be statistically insignificant, the anxiety is real. Jack knows the stories: a deaf youth walking the tracks and killed because he couldn't hear the train coming; cars and trucks hurrying to beat the train—and losing. According to Jack, the key is staying vigilant. Keeping people safe is his job. This responsibility is his vocation."

46. Unprotected/Kept Safe

Here is an image that is minor in the Epistles but that may be especially significant to people who have not been protected, particularly by someone who had or still has power over them. We think of victims of childhood sexual abuse, those who have suffered physically when no one was around who could or would protect them. Consider those who have felt unprotected because of traumatic events or unjust economic circumstances. How does one believe in a God who is Creator and protector when one's life experience tells a different story?

The First Letter of John provides words about grace in the image of Unprotected/Kept Safe: "The one who was born of God protects them, and the evil one does not touch them. We know that we are God's children, and that the whole world lies under the power of the evil one" (1 John 5:18–19). This protection is directly connected to the coming of the Son of God, Jesus Christ. When all else seems endlessly overwhelming—and, indeed, evil—by God's grace we know Christ who is "true," and we are in him who is "true" (1 John 5:20).

Even though to be called "children" of God may not connect with the daily lives of most adults, when people have been unprotected as children, the grace expressed in this image may be very good news. Likewise, this is a helpful image for children. "Little children, you are from God" (1 John 4:4). See what love God has given us, "that we should be called children of God; and that is what we are" (1 John 3:1). Also: "Everyone who believes that Jesus is the Christ has been born of God . . ." (1 John 5:1). And, finally, in Jude 1: "Jude, a servant of Jesus Christ . . . to those who are called, who are beloved in God . . . and kept safe for Jesus Christ."

- Have you ever felt unsafe, unprotected? Perhaps even now you feel this way. What are the circumstances? What does being kept safe through the grace of Jesus Christ mean to you? What could it mean?

- What about the neighbor next door, or the millions of neighbors around the world who have been left unprotected due to war, who are refugees, or who are continually exposed to dangers of another kind? What is the gospel word—and action—for them?

47. Judgment/Mercy

Judgment belongs to God. Yet so often people suffer unjustly because of the judgmental attitudes and actions of others, including the church itself. Mercy rests not in saying sin does not matter, and surely not in the absence of justice. Mercy rests in the unconditional love of God. This image of judgment and mercy acknowledges the judicial acts of God, knowing that we have not been condemned. In Jesus Christ's death God mercifully declares us innocent, even just; therefore we say with Paul that we are justified by grace through faith.

In Romans we find this image of judgment and mercy used most often. Paul writes, "Therefore you have no excuse, whoever you are, when you judge others; for in passing judgment on another you condemn yourself, because you, the judge, are doing the very same things" (2:1). No one will escape God's judgment: "There is no one who is righteous, not even one . . ." (3:10). All have sinned and are now justified by grace as a gift through the redemption that is in Christ Jesus (3:23). Jesus was "handed over to death for our trespasses and was raised for our justification" (4:25). Therefore, "since we are justified by faith, we have peace with God through our Lord Jesus Christ" (5:1). "There is therefore now no condemnation for those who are in Christ Jesus" (8:1). In an extensive passage, Rom 5:18–21, justification is spelled out fully, concluding with the words, "but where sin increased, grace abounded all the more, so that, just as sin exercised do-minion in death, so grace might also exercise dominion through justifica-tion leading to eternal life through Jesus Christ our Lord." Likewise, "It is God who justifies. Who is to condemn?" (8:33–34).

Mercy is God's work. Paul quotes God's words to Moses, "'I will have mercy on whom I have mercy,'" to which Paul adds, "So it depends not on human will or exertion, but on God who shows mercy" (Rom 9:14–16). These words from Titus add to our assurance: "But when the goodness and loving kindness of God our Savior appeared, he saved us, not because of any works of righteousness that we had done, but according to his mercy, through the water of rebirth and renewal by the Holy Spirit" (3:4–5). In the image of moving from "not a people" to being "God's people,"[1] we see the parallel of "once you had not received mercy, but now you have received mercy" (1 Pet 2:10). In 1 Tim 1:12–17 we see the writer grateful to Christ Jesus for having received mercy and for being judged faithful and appointed to his service. His having received mercy can serve as an encouragement for others who believe in Christ for eternal life.

The image of judgment is graphically portrayed in 1 Cor 4:1–5. Paul says "it is a very small thing" to be judged by "any human court"—in fact, he does not even judge himself, since "it is the Lord who judges me" (v. 4). Jesus Christ "is to judge the living and the dead" (2 Tim 4:1). Chris-tians are not to sue each other because only God judges (1 Cor 6:1–6). This same admonition is found in Rom 14:10–13, where Christians are asked, "Why do you pass judgment on your brother or sister?" and enjoined thus: "Let us therefore no longer pass judgment on one another . . ."

James warns against speaking evil against another or judging another (4:11) and assures that "the Lord is compassionate and merciful" (5:11). And in 1 Cor 11:29–33[2] we see, at the heart of the Lord's Supper, in which

---

1. Commented upon more extensively in the Not a People/God's People image in chapter 4

2. Commented upon more extensively in the Division/Unity image in chapter 4.

mercy is received in the body and blood of Christ, Christians judging one another by eating the Lord's Supper without concern for the others in the community.

In 1 Cor 6:11 the image of justification refers to the work of Christ in connection with other images: "But you were washed, you were sanctified, you were justified in the name of the Lord Jesus Christ and in the Spirit of our God." Surely the image of our being justified by faith is central for Christians. However, the Pauline Epistles use the image of judgment even more often in telling Christians not to judge one another. Having received God's mercy, the act of judging, which always belonged to God, now gives way to living together in grace and mercy. Our judgmental attitudes and actions are transformed by God's merciful grace into acts of justice in a world of inequality and injustice. Justification by grace through faith focuses our call to vocation in daily life. Mercy becomes more than pity. It is now strong, courageous justice-seeking.

The image of judgment is used in future terms—for example, "the God who stands ready to judge the living and the dead" (1 Pet 4:5–6, 17). Mercy, too, is an image for the end time: "Keep yourselves in the love of God; look forward to the mercy of our Lord Jesus Christ that leads to eternal life" (Jude 21).

Martin and Judgment for Life

Anita describes her time with Martin: "Martin retired from the state police a few years ago and now works a few days a month as a security guard at a neighboring town's courthouse. We spent a number of hours together over the course of several days. Martin is a man of faith and gives much time to service in his congregation. Earlier in life he had wrestled with pursuing pastoral ministry, but 'things just didn't work out that way.' Eventually he saw his calling as a state trooper as ministry.

"I saw in Martin's life the image of judgment and mercy. When I see a state trooper coming I always wonder, 'Do I have a headlight out? Is my speedometer wrong?' I am afraid of those who can issue tickets. However, in my time with Martin I realized that most troopers are not out to ruin a person's day. They are there to protect and serve. Martin spoke of judgment and mercy, not in those words, but in stories. Certainly he wrote his share of tickets, but his calling was to help make the roads safer. He desired mercy for all people that they might live another day.

"Martin takes seriously the gift of life given to us by God in Jesus Christ through the power of the Holy Spirit. I walked away with a sense of deep appreciation and newfound understanding of yet another way God partners with people for mission and ministry in the world. I asked him one more question: 'If I'm stopped by a cop on my way home, can I say I know you?' Martin answered, 'You could, but you'd probably get two tickets then.' Martin is grounded in grace, but it is not cheap grace. Trying to get out of a ticket by name-dropping would be cheap grace; so would grace without the love and mercy of God in Christ, saying such things as, 'Oh, Jesus has me covered,' so I can go on speeding (sinning). Thanks be to God for Martin."

- How does being justified by grace through faith change the way we think about mercy and transform us to seek justice for others and for the whole world?

- The Letters are concerned about judgmental attitudes and actions among Christians. How have you experienced these? How does living in God's mercy have the potential to curtail our judgment of others?

- Martin understands "cheap grace" and the necessity of just judgment. How is grace through the cross of Christ different from cheap grace?

48. Unloved/Loved

God is love, but what if we do not experience that love, either in our personal lives or in the church itself? To believe that we are unloved by others and even by God can be extremely painful. One may feel condemned, or alienated, or alone (all intersecting with other images in this book); whatever the particular manifestation, to be unloved is a dreadful state, and the very opposite of knowing the intimacy of God's unconditional love in Christ Jesus. Second Thessalonians 2:16–17 states so well the good news: "Now may our Lord Jesus Christ himself and God our Father, who loves us and through grace gave us eternal comfort and good hope, comfort your hearts and strengthen them in every good work and word."

Grace as God's love is absolutely connected to God's love flowing through God's beloved in their ministries in daily life. This longer passage from 1 John shows the embodiment of Christ's love: "Beloved, let us love one another, because love is from God; everyone who loves is born of God and knows God. Whoever does not love does not know God, for God is love. God's love was revealed among us in this way: God sent God's only Son into the world so that we might live through him.[3] In this is love, not that we loved God but that God loved us. . . . Beloved, since God loved us so much, we also ought to love one another" (4:7–11).

Without hope firmly grounded in God's love in Christ, we live in fear that we will not always be loved, or even liked. In fact, Scripture and our everyday lives reveal that we may often be objects of hatred. "Do not be astonished, brothers and sisters, that the world hates you. . . . We know love by this, that he [Jesus] laid down his life for us—and we ought to lay down our lives for one another. How does God's love abide in anyone who has the world's goods and sees a brother or sister in need and yet refuses help?" (1 John 3:13–17). Often within the church, particularly during periods of conflict, people become disillusioned when they discover that we are all capable of being unloving toward each other, even of hating one another. "Those who say, 'I love God,' and hate their brothers or sisters, are liars; for those who do not love a brother or sister whom they have seen, cannot love God whom they have not seen. . . . Those who love God must love their brothers and sisters also" (1 John 4:20–21).

Love is challenging. And yet this is our vocation; we are loved into action through Christ's death and resurrection: "Little children, let us love, not in word or speech, but in truth and action" (1 John 3:18). Love is kind. There is no fear in God's love in Christ: "There is no fear in love, but perfect love casts out fear; for fear has to do with punishment. . . . We love because God first loved us" (1 John 4:18–19). We pray that by grace we may move beyond our own lovelessness to embrace the limitless love of God in order to serve.

Finally, we have three familiar passages that deeply ground us in the grace of God's love: "You shall love your neighbor as yourself" (Gal 5:14); "Live in love, as Christ loved us and gave himself up for us" (Eph 5:2); and 1 Cor 13, which proceeds directly from the good news that we are the risen body of Christ (read the whole chapter!): "Love is patient; love is kind; love is not envious or boastful or arrogant or rude. It does not insist on its own way; it is not irritable or resentful; it does not rejoice in wrongdoing, but rejoices in the truth. It bears all things, believes all things, hopes all things, endures all things. Love never ends. . . . Now faith, hope, and love abide, these three; and the greatest of these is love."

---

3. The wording is similar to the very familiar gospel verse John 3:16.

Lynn and Chuck Loving God's Created Ones

From Aqisha's visit to Lynn and Chuck's place of vocation came this story: "Lynn and her husband, Chuck, live in a house on a hill, and their livelihood lies in the business of boarding and grooming dogs. After I arrived, I looked around and concluded this was not only their means of paying the bills; through their love and care for dogs, they have found a way to do ministry by loving and caring for people, loving all of God's creation.

"When I arrived, Lynn already had a small poodle on a table. At about 8:05, another car drove up. Lynn scurried back out into the office. Without a formal 'Good morning,' in a soft voice she said, 'How are things going?' The woman looked as if she would burst into tears and went on to tell about her seventeen-year-old son, who had suffered a knee injury in a football game. He had already been through multiple surgeries, and complications indicated that this was only the beginning of what would be a lifelong struggle. As the conversation continued, the woman handed her little dog, Banner, over to Lynn. Lynn cuddled Banner as the woman turned and went out the door to her car.

"During the day I became aware of the many moments of pain, some of which had become moments of grace, others of which had not. As I watched Lynn and Chuck work, I saw infinite patience, even when the dogs misbehaved. They love each dog for who the dog is. They know their customers, as they create a safe place for them to share what is going on in their lives even as they scurry and bustle about. Lynn and Chuck stop and listen when the customers speak. They embody the gospel message."

- What is it like to be unloved by another, by a community, by oneself? To feel unloved by God? Can you—do you—know the unconditional love of God in Christ Jesus?

- Is there a biblical text above which does or could shape the love of Christ you are able to share in your ministry in daily life, whatever that vocation may be?

49. Sins/Atoning Sacrifice

Romans 3:25 presents us with the image of atonement through blood: Christ Jesus, "whom God put forward as a sacrifice of atonement by his blood,[4] effective though faith." It goes on, "In his divine forbearance he had passed over the sins previously committed." This image of atonement, so prevalent in the Hebrew Scriptures, is used sparingly in the Epistles, with the exception of the book of Hebrews.

In Hebrews we read that Jesus "had to become like his brothers and sisters in every respect, so that he might be a merciful and faithful high priest in the service of God, to make a sacrifice of atonement for the sins of the people" (2:17). Jesus not only became the high priest, but "he entered once for all into the Holy Place, not with the blood of goats and calves, but with his own blood, thus obtaining eternal redemption. For if the blood of goats and bulls . . . sanctifies those who have been defiled so that their flesh is purified, how much more will the blood of Christ, who through the eternal Spirit offered himself without blemish to God, purify our conscience from dead works to worship the living God!" (9:12–14). "Nor was it to offer himself again and again, as the high priest enters the Holy Place year after year with blood that is not his own; for then he would have had to suffer again and again. . . . But as it is, he has appeared once for all at the end of the age to remove sin by the sacrifice of himself" (9:25–26). Similarly, in Heb 7:27 we read that "this he did once for all when he offered himself."

This atonement through Christ's offering his own self as a sacrifice is communal grace. And God will remember our sins no more: "'I will remember their sins and their lawless deeds no more.' Where there is forgiveness of these, there is no longer any offering for sin" (Heb 10:17–18). First John uses the image in a similar, complete, communal way. Jesus "is the atoning sacrifice for our sins, and not for ours only but also for the sins of the whole world" (2:2). And again, "In this is love, not that we loved God but that God loved us and sent the Son to be the atoning sacrifice for our sins" (4:10)

- Recall or read and review the Hebrew Scriptures in which the high priest made sacrifices for his own sins and for those of the people through the blood of sacrificial animals.

- How much different is it for Christ to become the high priest who has become the once-for-all sacrifice for us and for all? What does it mean to you to be "at one" with God (atonement)?

---

4. The blood of Jesus is mentioned throughout the Epistles in connection with a number of images. In relation to this particular image, in addition to Rom 3:25, see Rom 5:9; Eph 1:7; Col 1:20.

50. Stained/Cleansed

Human beings sometimes stay away from holy things, holy people, the holy God because they consider themselves stained, unclean, and therefore unworthy of being in the presence of the holy. Likewise, we may think of others—individuals or whole groups of people—as dirty, less "clean," thus creating a dividing line of exclusion. In essence, we are all stained by sin, and this image is found in the Epistles—for example, "The tongue is placed among our members as a world of iniquity; it stains the whole body . . ." (Jas 3:6).

The image of grace is that we have been cleansed, washed, made clean through Jesus Christ. Paul enumerates the "stains" or sins of the Corinthians and then goes on to say, "And this is what some of you used to be. But you were washed, you were sanctified, you were justified in the name of the Lord Jesus Christ and in the Spirit of our God" (1 Cor 6:11).[5] And in First John we read that "the blood of Jesus, God's son, cleanses us from all sin" (1:7).

Hebrews uses this image to emphasize that, in contrast to the sacrifices offered year after year according to the first covenant, because "Christ came into the world" worshipers have been "cleansed once for all" (10:5, 2). No stain remains. "Therefore, my friends, since we have confidence to enter the sanctuary by the blood of Jesus . . . let us approach with a true heart in full assurance of faith, with our hearts sprinkled clean from an evil conscience and our bodies washed with water. Let us hold fast to the confession of our hope without wavering, for he who has promised is faithful" (10:19, 22–23).

Paul in Romans 14 goes on at length about not judging those whom we would think of as stained, made unclean by what they eat. Our faith practices and observances, the things in which we engage or from which we abstain, do not in themselves stain us or keep us clean. "I know and am persuaded in the Lord Jesus that nothing is unclean in itself; but it is unclean for anyone who thinks it unclean" (14:14). Once again the image is communal. Paul is insistent: "Do not, for the sake of food, destroy the work of God. Everything is indeed clean, but it is wrong for you to make others fall by what you eat . . ." (14:20).

Being cleansed is the work of the Spirit in Jesus Christ, the work of justification and sanctification. "For God did not call us to impurity but in

---

5. "Washing" is of course connected with baptism, the image explored in chapter 4

holiness" (1 Thess 4:7). This cleansing makes us "pure" and "holy," not to be set apart from the world but to be placed more deeply into it, into those situations stained by ongoing systemic sin, the complex injustice in which we, too, participate. Christ died once and for all. Our stains are no longer indelible; however, new stains appear daily. Cleansing is a gift that we might live faithfully, serving, loving, and caring in daily life.

- What stains do you carry with you? What stains of other people keep you at a distance?

- How do you relate to the word "holy"? By being both sinner and saint, both stained and cleansed in Christ Jesus, how can we now relate to all kinds of people as created and loved by God?

51. Shamed/Unashamed

Matt the Bank Teller

Erik, having walked with Matt, tells this story: "Matt is single, in his late twenties, a college graduate who works as a teller at a local bank. He said, 'I've been with the bank three years now and really like what I do most of the time, but I can't see being a teller the rest of my life. I'd like to move into financial planning and work my way up to management.'

"'Even now as a teller,' he said, 'I've heard my share of sad stories. I mean, one of the most tragic things we see is people who go into foreclosure or who have to declare bankruptcy, and they're just so distraught and hopeless. Maybe they made poor life choices, or maybe something awful happened to them beyond their control and their lives are falling apart.'

"Matt said he sees a loss of pride and self-worth. 'Financial matters—money in general—is such a personal and sensitive topic for many people that losing money, not being able to take care of one's self or family, carries a sense of personal shame and to some degree social shame.' As a teller he cannot change their financial situation, but Matt believes he is poised to be a Christ-image to these people by looking at them in a way that still affirms their dignity and their worth, to help them ride through that sense of shame, offering compassion to rise out of the ashes."

Shame

Shame is a deeply rooted human emotion and reality. Many people live their entire lives under the burden of shame, laid upon them by harsh words from their childhood, by life experiences, or by judgmental authorities. It is deeper than not being "good enough." It sometimes becomes the essence of their very being. Therefore this image, so little used in speaking of sin and grace, can be a powerful way to reach the dark place of the shamed self. The strong Word of grace can meet people at this deep place. Let us look to Jesus, "who for the sake of the joy that was set before him endured the cross, disregarding its shame, and has taken his seat at the right hand of the throne of God" (Heb 12:2). Jesus bore our shame. And Paul, quoting Scripture, writes, "No one who believes in him will be put to shame" (Rom 9:33; 10:11).

Shame is associated with hiding: "We have renounced the shameful things that one hides; we refuse to practice cunning or to falsify God's word . . ." (2 Cor 4:2). We do not merely by ourselves suddenly become unashamed. The preceding verse makes clear that it is grace alone that frees us for ministry in daily life: "Therefore, since it is by God's mercy that we are engaged in this ministry, we do not lose heart" (2 Cor 4:1).

By grace we are liberated from the effects of shame, even though insults still sting. "For Christ did not please himself; but, as it is written, 'The insults of those who insult you have fallen on me'" (Rom 15:3). By grace we are liberated from being ashamed of one another and of the Word itself: "Do not be ashamed, then, of the testimony about our Lord or of me his prisoner, but join with me in suffering for the gospel, relying on the power of God, who saved us and called us with a holy calling. . . . I am not ashamed, for I know the one in whom I have put my trust. . ." (2 Tim 1:8–9, 12). Paul also holds an expectation and hope that "I will not be put to shame in any way, but that by my speaking with all boldness, Christ will be exalted now as always in my body, whether by life or by death" (Phil 1:20). "God chose what is foolish in the world to shame the wise; God chose what is weak in the world to shame the strong" (1 Cor 1:27).[6]

God makes salvation "perfect through sufferings" for many "children," and we are thereby connected: "Jesus is not ashamed to call them brothers and sisters" (Heb 2:10–11). Shame may still cling closely to human beings,

---

6. See chapter 2 for the image of Unenlightened/Wise and chapter 3 for the image of Weakness/Strength.

but in Christ we already are released, and therefore we live in a new reality of Christ's being unashamed of us and of our being unashamed of ourselves or one another.

- What "clinging" effects of shame have you experienced or seen in others? Did the effects linger for a short time or a long time?

- How does the Christ who bore our shame enter our vulnerability and release us, thus providing the potential for being unashamed of ourselves or one another?

52. Labor/Rest

Is work part of creation or part of the fall (Gen 2)? I believe it is helpful to talk about holy work and Sabbath rest.[7] Part of the human predicament, however, is twofold: 1) that we think we may be saved by our own labor, or 2) that the labor of our vocation in daily life becomes burdensome, even oppressive under unjust systems of economic inequality. Suffering results. Some people labor their entire lives without hope. Others go without opportunities for work.

Labor/Rest is a minor image in the Epistles, but a major part of Christians' daily lives. Paul a number of times refers to Christians working together—for example, "we are workers with you for your joy, because you stand firm in the faith" (2 Cor 1:24). The work may be full of struggle, even persecution and suffering, but in this new life together in Christ, being workers together itself is grace.

In the Hebrew Scriptures one finds a number of passages about the good news of rest. In Gen 2:2–3 we read that the Creator God "finished the work" and "rested on the seventh day . . ." And God blessed and hallowed the seventh day because God rested from all the work done in creation. This image, from the beginning, places every kind of work in our daily lives within God's creation. Rest is gift. And God invites us into that gift so that work can become calling.

---

7. See Norma Cook Everist and Craig L. Nessan, *Transforming Leadership* (Minneapolis: Fortress, 2008) 149–59.

Betty Who Rests in Her Labor

Michelle listens to Betty and shares her story: "I pulled into the familiar driveway next to the house, walked up the sidewalk and rang the doorbell. Betty had been a friend of my family for as long as I could remember. She lived across the street from the house I grew up in. Betty was handpicked out of her graduating high school class some sixty years ago by her small town's only lawyer to work as his secretary. As the years went on she developed a reputation as a sharp and savvy administrator and accountant and eventually started her own tax business on the side, which would grow to include most of the county. Seven years ago at seventy-five Betty decided to finally retire (her husband of fifty-four years had retired twenty years earlier), but she continued her tax service from home. She frequently says, 'It's not work when you love what you do, and I love what I do!'

"Six months ago Betty lost her husband, Jim, to cancer on his eighty-fourth birthday. As we sat at her kitchen table, sharing a cup of coffee, she explained that the house seems quiet and empty now, but she continues with her tax work. 'It's like solving puzzles.' Some of her clients represent large farm corporations. Another client she had for many years would just throw all of his receipts and statements into a brown paper bag and give it to her to sort out. Rather than be frustrated or angry, Betty welcomes the challenges, seeing them as 'a grand puzzle to solve.' She added, 'The thing with numbers is they always work out. There is always a solution.'

"Betty also talked about how her clients had become her friends. As she would sit with them in her basement office, talking through their finances, she learned about things that did not always have a solution: pending divorces, financial struggles, unwed daughter's pregnancies, cancer treatments and drinking problems. Over the years Betty had become much more than a tax accountant for this small community. And the community had become much more to her.

"'I would like to show you something,' Betty said. She left the kitchen and returned with a very large book that looked like a photo album. 'This is a book I made of all the cards and notes and memorials that I received when Jim died. There are over two hundred of them.' I just listened as Betty walked me through her memory book. It was a holy moment. Jim was at rest. In some ways Betty's form of ministry has given her peace; her labor has become her rest and her 'clients' her partners in Christ, now, and when she, too, finally ceases her labor."

The writer to the Hebrews, who calls the Hebrew people (and us) "brothers and sisters, holy partners in a heavenly calling" (3:1) and "partners of Christ" (3:14), has us wrestle with being part of God's rest. "Therefore, while the promise of entering his rest is still open, let us take care that none of you should seem to have failed to reach it" (4:1). Those "who formerly received the good news failed to enter . . ." (4:6). The image is limited but clear—there is still an open invitation to the gospel, and this good news is portrayed as "rest." "For those who enter God's rest also cease from their labors as God did . . ." (4:10).

- In what ways and for whom is labor part of the suffering of humankind? Where is that suffering most noticeable?

- How is "resting" from labor and being part of God's rest good news for you, for your Sabbath, your spirituality, your life now and into eternity?

53. Inertia/Standing, Walking

Bud Walking in the Spirit

Seth describe his experience walking with Bud: "As I put on my clear safety classes, Bud Larson explained how the shift foreman gave special permission for me to spend the day at World Painting Solutions where Bud runs a plasma-cutting table. The smell of heat and burning metal filled the warehouse; molten metal sparks broke up the yellow tint of industrial lighting around the shop. As the day went on I helped Bud with his work of moving parts, tagging items and sorting steel to be discarded. By the end of the day I was exhausted and dirty. I could not imagine waking up the next day to attend to the list of orders awaiting Bud. But he gave it his all and did it with pleasure. His positive energy and feelings of accomplishment overwhelmed me.

"Bud believed God opened doors for him at World Painting. He knew he mattered and had a sense of hope in his physical work. He didn't join in the 'men's locker room talk' of sexually harassing speech I heard throughout the day. I noticed a sizeable piece of metal that he had cut and hung on the wall above his computer: a cross cut from scrap, with a heart cut out of the inside; it was in view of everyone who came wanting parts cut from Bud's plasma table. Bud said, 'That is the center of my day, and of my life.' Bud has a way of walking in the Spirit that is contagious. Forgiven and claimed, with a smile on his face and hospitality in his heart, Bud, in this factory setting, seems to punch the clock with a different beat."

Energizing Christians

Romans 8:4 describes the Christ event as energizing Christians to "walk not according to the flesh but according to the Spirit." Romans 5 begins with the important "therefore" and continues "since we are justified by faith, we have peace with God through our Lord Jesus Christ, through whom we have obtained access to this grace in which we stand" (vv. 1–2). Likewise, "Now I would remind you, brothers and sisters, of the good news that I proclaimed to you, which you in turn received, in which also you stand, through which also you are being saved" (1 Cor 15:1–2). "Standing" or "walking" can be important images of soteriology for twenty-first-century Christians, particularly young people who seek action in their life's journey. These images give a sense of purpose and direction for individuals stuck in inertia and congregations mired in apathy.

There is a warning with this image—"So if you think you are standing, watch out that you do not fall" (1 Cor 10:12)—which is quickly followed by how common it is that Christians are tested in their faith. God is faithful and will not let us be tested beyond our strength. Perhaps that applies also to our standing up and walking forth in faith. Our faithful God provides the strength: "We walk by faith" (2 Cor 5:7). God's faith lives in and through us. And we stand in God's presence, not being mere "peddlers of God's word" but speakers and people of action and sincerity "sent from God" (2 Cor 2:17). Jude 24: "To God who is able to keep you from falling, and to make you stand without blemish in the presence of God's glory rejoicing. . ."

As we move from inertia toward action, John, who is all about "abiding in," which could be misinterpreted as static, says, "Whoever says, 'I abide in [Jesus],' ought to walk just as he walked" (1 John 2:6). This "walking" needs to be "in the light" not in "darkness," so that there be no cause for stumbling, either for oneself or the brother or sister whom one is called to love (1 John 2:9–11). We are called by grace to walk also in love and in truth: "I was overjoyed to find some of your children walking in the truth . . ." (2 John 4–6); "I have no greater joy than this, to hear that my children are walking in the truth" (3 John 4).

The two go together: standing and walking. By grace we can and are to stand fast in the true grace of God (1 Pet 5:12); as Peter writes, "Prepare your minds for action . . . set all your hope on the grace that Jesus Christ will bring you . . ." (1 Pet 1:13).

- When do you think about your daily life as merely one of inertia? And of your faith as static?

- Even if you have difficulty in physically standing or walking, how have you seen or experienced a brother or sister in Christ, a whole faith community, or you yourself standing firm in the faith and "walking" in hope, strengthened for daily work in the world?

CHAPTER 7

People Transformed to Be Change Agents in the World

By grace through faith we are saved from our own self-justification, boastfulness, and self-deprecation. Works flow from faith, empowering us to be change agents in the world. We are clothed in Christ and are invited to "put on the Lord Jesus Christ." Grace is a treasure God richly provides us; therefore we are to set our hopes on God. A theology of the cross and resurrection means walking with the Christ who walks with those who suffer economically. "It's all about power," some say, but Christ relinquished power and died a lowly death in order to transform power itself. We now become powerful servants. The battle with evil has been definitively won through Jesus Christ's death and resurrection.

Many people are concerned that because of their human nature they are not good enough for God. Christ humbly entered this human nature and through the cross we have become servants of Christ. Who wants to look like a coward or seem foolish? God did not give us a spirit of cowardice, but rather a spirit of strength and of love. The image of Loser/Victorious begs the question, over whom or what is Jesus victorious? And who is the loser? God gives the victory to us *through* Jesus, but not to conquer. When people or nations are disconnected and cannot reconcile their differences, they need a mediator. Christ is the mediator between God and humankind.

54. Boastfulness/Works

Gifts are used for works, and works are needed to carry out our vocations in daily life. However, Christians are not saved by their works: "[Our Savior] saved us, not because of any works of righteousness that we had done, but according to his mercy, through the water of rebirth and renewal by the Holy Spirit" (Titus 3:5). And, "For by grace you have been saved through faith, and this is not your own doing; it is the gift of God—not the result of works, so that no one may boast" (Eph 2:8). The problem lies not in doing works but in boasting about those works—in other words, idolatry: "so that no one might boast in the presence of God . . . Let the one who boasts, boast in the Lord" (1 Cor 1:29–31; see also 2 Cor 10:17).

Now boasting, as often as it is mentioned in the Epistles, may not be the presenting problem. The central problem more likely is self-justification before God, making ourselves look good in comparison with others, trying to gain prestige and honor in the church and in the world. We cannot justify ourselves before God; trying to do so causes not only divisions, but oppression and human suffering. On the other hand, believing one has no gifts for works of ministry, self-deprecation, denies the work of the Creator God and the work of the Spirit in the very ones for whom Christ died and rose.[1] In either case, the human predicament is unbelief. The good news is that by grace we are not only saved for eternal life but also empowered by the Spirit to be at work in the world in Christlike ways.

Brenda on the Oncology Unit

After walking with Brenda, Jason tells this story: "Brenda is a nurse supervisor for the third floor oncology unit at Our Redeemer Hospital, a midsized facility serving three towns in Illinois. The day of our visit was grey and cool. Brenda met me at the front desk at 8:00 a.m. and we started on our way. We visited with the chaplains in the chapel and then talked in her office before she needed to do rounds with her staff. We talked about her vocation. She said her grandmother tells a story about Brenda starting to hear her call to nursing at age two, when she would bring bandages or drinks to family members who were sick. Not long after that she started taking appointments in her doctor book for her basement play hospital. She truly sees her work today as a call from God by serving in the world.

1. The work of feminist and liberation theologians has made this clear.

"The human predicament in the hospital varies in shape and scope, but it is almost always tied to human frailty in its multiple forms. Our Redeemer's nurses are committed to excellence but not for excellence's sake; rather they work 'towards holistic care through collaboration and innovation,' according to Brenda. I found grace in their work instead of boastfulness. Many of the nurses had had experiences of patient recovery that defy understanding, and almost across the board these are attributed to God's action. When we talked about this, Brenda told me how the staff opens their award ceremonies and development days with reflection or prayer. She added how they often start their meetings with what they call 'quick win,' a positive reflection on what is going well. It was clear that there was a strong connection to these positive experiences and God's saving grace at work."

Bold Ministry and Mission

Christ is the source of life and of ministry and of our being change agents in the world. Paul boasts of the eagerness of the early Christians' ministry and of the apostle's own behavior in the world, which is frank and godly and sincere, not by earthly wisdom but "by the grace of God" (2 Cor 1:12). He defends boasting, and yet sees it as problematic: "No one will deprive me of my ground for boasting! If I proclaim the gospel, this gives me no ground for boasting, for an obligation is laid on me, and woe to me if I do not proclaim the gospel!" (1 Cor 9:15–16). One is not to boast "beyond limits, that is, in the labors of others, but our hope is that as your faith increases, our sphere of action among you may be greatly enlarged, so that we may proclaim the good news in lands beyond you . . ." (2 Cor 10:15–16). Throughout 2 Cor 11–12 Paul talks about boasting many times, not according to "human standards" (11:18) but on behalf of bold ministry and mission, and then, in connection with his own weakness: "If I must boast, I will boast of the things that show my weakness" (11:30).[2] Boasting is not without ambiguity even when it is transformed by grace for work for Christ.

Romans makes it clear that we cannot boast in the law or the works of the law (2:17, 23; 4:2). "Then what becomes of boasting? It is excluded. By what law? By that of works? No, but by the law of faith. For we hold that a person is justified by faith apart from works prescribed by the law" (3:27–28). "If Abraham was justified by works, he has something to boast

2. Note the image of Weakness/Strength in chapter 3.

about, but not before God" (4:2). Paul goes on, saying, "it depends on faith in order that the promise may rest on grace" (4:16), and, "Therefore, since we are justified by faith, we have peace with God through our Lord Jesus Christ . . . and we boast in our hope of sharing the glory of God" (5:1–2).

Paul says that not only do we have peace with God, "but we boast in our sufferings, knowing that suffering produces endurance, and endurance produces character, and character produces hope, and hope does not disappoint us" (5:3–5). Also, "We ourselves boast of you among the churches of God for your steadfastness and faith during all your persecutions and the afflictions that you are enduring" (2 Thess 1:4).

"We even boast in God through our Lord Jesus Christ, through whom we have now received reconciliation" (Rom 5:11). We also cannot boast in our religious heritage (whether Jew or Greek—or a particular denomination or ethnic background today). "Do not boast over the branches. If you do boast, remember that it is not you that support the root, but the root that supports you" (Rom 11:18). It is all by grace through faith!

Paul also warns against boasting about certain leaders. "So let no one boast about human leaders. For all things are yours, whether Paul or Apollos or Cephas or the world or life or death or the present or the future—all belong to you, and you belong to Christ, and Christ belongs to God" (1 Cor 3:21–23). A few verses later he is concerned that "none of you will be puffed up in favor of one against another. . . . What do you have that you did not receive? And if you received it, why do you boast as if it were not a gift?" (1 Cor 4:6–7). But he also often boasts about Christians who are at work in their lives of faith, often in circumstances of uncertainty: "I die every day! That is as certain, brothers and sisters, as my boasting of you—a boast that I make in Christ Jesus our Lord" (1 Cor 15:31).

The human predicament, in its many forms and ambiguities, continues; however, works do flow from faith. Our Lord "saved us and called us with a holy calling, not according to our works, but according to his own purpose and grace" (2 Tim 1:8–9). That cannot be disputed in the Epistles, and there are passages and stories beyond what are given here that show these works of grace. "May I never boast of anything except the cross of our Lord Jesus Christ, by which the world has been crucified to me, and I to the world" (Gal 6:14).

James sees the problem with boasting: "If you have bitter envy and selfish ambition in your hearts, do not be boastful and false to the truth" (3:14). Just a verse earlier he writes of the importance of works: "Show by your good life that your works are done with gentleness born of wisdom" (3:13). He says that "God opposes the proud, but gives grace to the humble" (4:6)[3] and is clear in writing, "Let the believer who is lowly boast in being raised up" (1:9). The Letter of James makes it very clear that works are an essential gift of grace: "What good is it, my brothers and sisters, if you say you have faith, but do not have works: can faith save you? If a brother or sister is naked and lacks daily food, and one of you says to them, 'Go in peace; keep warm and eat your fill,' and yet you do not supply their bodily needs, what is the good of that? So faith by itself, if it has not works, is dead. But someone will say, 'You have faith and I have works.' Show me your faith apart from your works, and I by my works will show you my faith" (2:14–18).

- How do you see either boasting or self-deprecation as human predicaments from which we and the church need saving? How do you see either in yourself?

- What are some of the many manifestations of boasting in heritage, or in certain leaders, that are idolatrous, often dividing the church? How can we address the problems of basing faith on these?

- By grace through faith we are saved. How have you seen works flowing from faith, being a witness to faith and making a real difference in the lives of people and the world itself?

55. Unclothed/Clothed

Evelyn Clothing Her Sisters

Mindy makes a visit to Evelyn and tells her story: "Evelyn looked up from her work and greeted me with a big smile as I entered her beauty shop. It wasn't the hairstyles that caught my eye, but the pink. Evelyn wears pink proudly as a survivor of breast cancer. It was a joy to watch her work. Somehow she manages to remember conversations from each client's last visit and keep those conversations going while her fingers are busy combing and trimming. It's like watching an artist working on a sculpture.

"On November 22, 2005, Evelyn's life changed when, during a routine exam, she was diagnosed with breast cancer. She acknowledges it might return. She shares her story and works with her gifts to help others battling

3. Quoting Prov 3:34.

cancer. The best gift is her time and talent for helping women who have lost their hair through chemo and radiation. She shared a story from a month before.

"The sister of a cancer patient wanted to buy and have a wig fitted for her sister, but the cancer patient was showing no interest. Evelyn suggested that the sisters come in and they could look and just talk. They came and Evelyn said they all had such a fun time laughing and trying on wigs. At the end of the visit the woman did order a wig. A few days later, while reading the newspaper, Evelyn saw an obituary for the woman for whom she had fitted that wig. She called the sister to confirm and console. Quite a shock, since only a few days earlier they all had been laughing together.

"About a month later the wig arrived. Evelyn assured the sister that it could be returned, but the sister wanted to donate the wig to someone else to use, someone who could not afford one. I thought about Evelyn's story and her work and of Jesus' words, 'I was naked and you gave me clothing.' Hair is so much of who we are. Evelyn knows that."

Being Clothed with Christ

"As many of you as were baptized into Christ have clothed yourself with Christ" (Gal 3:27). Putting a white garment on the newly baptized is a symbol. But it is not just symbolic. It is an image of soteriology, of what Christ actually does. Hebrews uses the image of nakedness before God: "No creature is hidden, but all are naked and laid bare to the eyes of the one to whom we must render an account" (4:13). In our nakedness, shame, lack of identity, lack of being, Christ places himself on us. We are clothed in Christ. In the new life as believers we are invited to "put on the Lord Jesus Christ . . ."

This is God's action of grace, and yet the wording is often to "clothe yourselves." In Jesus you were taught "to clothe yourselves with the new self, created according to the likeness of God in true righteousness and holiness" (Eph 4:24). The old self is gone: "You have stripped off the old self with its practices and have clothed yourselves with the new self. . . . In that renewal there is no longer Greek and Jew, circumcised and uncircumcised, barbarian, Scythian, slave and free; but Christ is all and in all!" (Col 3:9–11). Once again, grace is communal and removes all divisions.

What does this new clothing look like? "As God's chosen ones, holy and beloved, clothe yourselves with compassion, kindness, humility, meekness and patience" (Col 3:12). We are to forgive as Christ has forgiven us. "Above all, clothe yourselves with love, which binds everything together in perfect harmony" (Col 3:14). Finally, "All of you must clothe yourselves with humility in your dealings with one another. . ." (1 Pet 5:5).

In 2 Cor 5:1–4 Paul mixes images, writing of the "earthly tent" in which we live and our "longing to be clothed with our heavenly dwelling."[4] But he goes on, "if indeed, when we have taken it off we will not be found naked . . . because we wish not to be unclothed but to be further clothed, so that what is mortal may be swallowed up by life."

Being clothed is more than an image: "To the present hour we are hungry and thirsty, we are poorly clothed and beaten and homeless, and we grow weary from the work of our own hands. When reviled, we bless; when persecuted, we endure; when slandered, we speak kindly" (1 Cor 4:11–13). We cannot glibly speak mere words to someone who is suffering, saying, "All is fine." Throughout the centuries Christians have clothed—not to mention fed and housed—millions who were "unclothed," while they themselves have taken comfort in being "clothed" in Christ. The challenge continues with the homeless, hungry, and unclothed—with all that might mean—among us.

- Have you ever felt naked, without clothing, before God? What does it mean to you not only to be clothed *by* Christ, but *with* Christ?

- How might we together as agents of Christ clothe those in need in the world?

56. Poverty/Riches

In 2 Tim 1 the gospel is described as the grace given to us in Christ Jesus; we are to "guard the good treasure entrusted" to us "with the help of the Holy Spirit living in us" (1:14). Grace is a treasure of riches God "richly provides us" and therefore we are to set our hopes on God rather than on the uncertainty of earthly riches. This "treasure" is a good foundation for the future so that we "may take hold of the life that really is life." This includes being "rich in good works, generous, and ready to share" (1 Tim 6:17–19).

---

4. At first glance this image could be included under Image 34, A Servant in the House/The House Itself, except that the context makes clear Paul is talking about the body, not a building.

Similarly, in Phil 4:19 we read that "God will fully satisfy every need of yours . . ." This is directly connected to the grace of Christ Jesus, which is described as "riches"—but not earthly riches, because in the previous chapter Paul says, "Whatever gains I had, these I have come to regard as loss because of Christ. More than that, I regard everything as loss because of the surpassing value of knowing Christ Jesus my Lord" (3:7–8). Paul has suffered loss "of all things" but regards them as "rubbish, in order that I may gain Christ. . ." (v. 8). Poverty here is not poverty as we think of it but being without the treasure of grace.

Key in this soteriological image is 2 Cor 8:9: "For you know the generous act of our Lord Jesus Christ, that though he was rich, yet for your sakes he became poor, so that by his poverty you might become rich." Christ thereby embraces all of the world's poverty, and takes it into himself. He takes it to the cross so that in the resurrection we might have this treasure of life in Christ, not to become wealthy in the world, but to receive a generous heart, a giving spirit, and a transformed life of caring for those who are poor.

This is the very opposite of a "prosperity" gospel, based on a theology of glory that is all about "me," "my personal salvation," and "my gaining all the wealth that I can." James does not go easy on the rich: "The rich will disappear like a flower in the field. For the sun rises with its scorching heat and withers the field; its flower falls, and its beauty perishes. It is the same way with the rich; in the midst of a busy life, they will wither away" (Jas 1:10–11). In chapter 5 he demonstrates his concern for those who suffer economic injustice: "Come now, you rich people, weep and wail for the miseries that are coming to you. . . . Your riches have rotted. . . . You have laid up treasure for the last days. Listen! The wages of the laborers who mowed your fields, which you kept back by fraud, cry out, and the cries of the harvesters have reached the ears of the Lord of hosts" (5:1–4).

A theology of the cross and resurrection means walking with the Christ who walks with those who suffer economically. This Epistle image is about caring for people living in poverty and the generosity of God activating our own generosity. Paul is direct in his Letters to the Corinthians. "Already you have all you want!" (1 Cor 4:8). Paul also lavishly praises those who have given: "We want you to know, brothers and sisters, about the grace of God that has been granted to the churches of Macedonia; for during a severe ordeal of affliction, their abundant joy and their extreme poverty have overflowed in a wealth of generosity on their part. For, as I can testify, they voluntarily gave according to their means, and even beyond their means, begging us earnestly for the privilege of sharing in this ministry to the saints. . ." (2 Cor 8:1–4).

Throughout the centuries and today, Christians together, by the grace of God in Christ Jesus, have been able to make a difference in the world through giving to relieve poverty. We also are called to be advocates for changing inequitable economic systems that keep poor people poor and make rich people more wealthy. Second Corinthians 8 and 9 build on that key verse, "For you know the generous act of our Lord Jesus Christ, that though he was rich, yet for your sakes he became poor, so that by his poverty you might become rich" (8:9). The "you" is plural. Paul speaks about one group's "present abundance" and another's "need" and of giving in order "that there may be a fair balance" (8:13–14). The transformation in Christ results in "eagerness" of generosity (v. 16), "cheerful givers" (9:7), multiplication of increase in the harvest of righteousness, and "ministry that not only supplies the needs of the saints but also overflows with many thanksgiving to God" (9:10–12). And all of this "because of the surpassing grace of God" and God's "indescribable gift" (9:14–15).

- If Christ became poor that we might become rich, how does that transform us so that in Christ's embrace of all the world's poor, we are empowered to work for economic justice?

- How is Christ growing your generous heart?

Serge from Kenya

Mamy shares a story of God at work in the world: "Serge and his wife, Olivia, laypersons with the W.B. Translators ministry, are in the United States for three months, visiting with their partner churches. They now work in collaboration with the people of the Democratic Republic of Congo using French and Kiswahili to help them translate the Bible into tribal languages. We became acquainted when we were in Kenya.

"Serge had been a computer analyst with a global financial institution in Madagascar, my home country. He had gone to a private college and was well paid in his job with the financial institution, but he and his wife had a desire to serve others using their gifts. He would not go easily to that journey. He shared that leaving behind what he knew for something that he was not sure about was a daily challenge and a daily reminder of the need to trust God in his life. Serge said, 'Although this is not a fancy, well-paid job, and sometimes we face hardship of travels in and out of Congo, we feel an inner peace in helping others through God's work in daily life. Whatever I have now is not because I deserve it, but because of God's grace alone.'

"Serge is confident that his successful career with the global financial institution in Madagascar was part of his formation to help him in his current work. He also feels freed from the strings of his well-paid job. Our conversation went on to explore how God is at work in the world, and our asking how we join God as part of God's mission in the world."

57. Lower/Higher

Power—it's all about power. Whether we live and work in a patriarchal, hierarchal system or not, who is higher and who is lower in any system is related to the power of money, of status, of race, of heritage, of education, of . . . Fill in the blank. Even in a so-called classless society, inequality remains. Some are higher and some are lower, and for many people, opportunities for this to change remain elusive.

But were we created to be so? Were some created to rule over others and some relegated to lower-class status by "nature"? Inequality is an ongoing facet of the human predicament. We discover a few Epistle passages using this image, both acknowledging it and directly relating it to the work of Christ on the cross. In the Letter to the Hebrews we are encouraged to not neglect so great a salvation; it speaks of signs, wonders, angels, and the Holy Spirit and what we do not yet see, "but we do see Jesus, who for a little while was made lower than the angels, now crowned with glory and honor because of the suffering of death, so that by the grace of God he might taste death for everyone" (2:9). It is clear that God is the higher power and that Christ relinquished such high power to die a lowly death, not so that only some should be powerful, wealthy, dominant, but so that his death and resurrection would be for everyone, people of every class and kind, opening up opportunities to serve across the world's demarcations of power.

Diana and Campus Ministry

Serving as campus minister at a large state-related university for nineteen years, Diana works on behalf of a denominational ministry in an interfaith center that is owned and run by the university. Faithfully she serves by walking with students with their own questions about faith, life goals, and discernment of vocation.

For decades the university of 42,000 had been a national football powerhouse because of past glories and its beloved coach. They put trust in their tradition and their godlike heroes. And then that idealism, their very belief system, was shaken to the core by the scandal that rocked the campus in the heart of football season. One in power had violated the most vulnerable by sexual abuse. Subsequently, others in power made choices to protect the football program rather than protect and aid the victims. When the news broke, the national media was everywhere.

Diana herself was full of questions about her ministry at that time of crisis. In the first days, students who had themselves suffered abuse at some point in their lives needed ministry. There was so much to absorb as the scandal unfolded. When the semester came to an end, people just wanted a chance to catch their breath. At the beginning of the new semester, Diana asked herself, "Who needs ministry now?" How does a whole institution change course when powerful programs and people seemed untouchable?

Diana took a chance. For years she had ministered in small circles within that huge institution, keeping to her appointed place. But then she discerned needs beyond this circle. Just before yet another legal hearing, she sent a note to a university vice president whose work was in the midst of the scandal, saying she cared about him and his vocation. She sent more notes to others in high places.

When football is demystified and people's failings are made public, how do we go on without feeding on our own illusions? Diana knew that Christ, "though he was in the form of God, did not regard equality with God as something to be exploited," and that "being found in human form, he humbled himself and became obedient to the point of death—even death on a cross" (Phil 2:5–8). When the institutions, programs, and people in whom we put our ultimate trust fall, we can look to Jesus, who, for a little while, was made lower than the angels.

In the midst of humiliation rather than honor, what is the call to servant ministry among the lowly and among those in the highest places? Diana knew as she wrapped her arms around those whose tears were close. And she knew, too, when she received a note from a university office she had never dared to enter before that read, "Thank you. Your prayers help more than you realize."

The Mind of Christ

So we have those amazing words that begin the "mind of Christ" passage of Phil 2: "Though he was in the form of God, [Christ Jesus] did not regard equality with God as something to be exploited, but emptied himself . . ." (vv. 6–7).[5] Because Christ emptied himself, humbled himself, no human being need remain in a lower state. And no human being has the right to make another feel humiliated, or empty, or lower. We are now one in Christ, raised with him. Humility itself has been transformed. Our humility is because we have all been raised in Christ. "Humble yourselves before the Lord, and God will exalt you" (Jas 4:10).

- How do you consider yourself in regard to class or status in the world? How do you consider others? What is the resulting relationship?

- To what servant ministries, in high and low places, are you called by the Christ who refused to exploit power but took the form of a servant?

- What possibilities for making a more equitable society come directly from Christ's lowering himself so that all might be raised with him?

58. Evil/Evil Conquered

The concept of evil *per se* is rarely mentioned in North American society today. Neither is it mentioned extensively in the Epistles. One often hears the word used when a horrendous crime has been committed and the media describe the perpetrator as "evil," perhaps because it is hard for most people to believe that the propensity to do evil is present in all human beings and not just certain "evil" people. Evil has been present in the world from the beginning, and it remains today in our war-torn, inhumane world. This is indeed the human predicament. Throughout Scripture evil is connected to sin and to the devil. So how is it used in the Epistles, after the death and resurrection of Christ?

In the First Letter of John, in a series of "I am writing to you because" statements, we read, "I am writing to you, young people, because you have conquered the evil one" (2:13). There is repetition and an addition in verse 14: "because you are strong and the word of God abides in you and you

---

5. The Phil 2 passage also was used in chapter 2, Double-Minded/Singled-Minded, to emphasize the "mind" of Christ. Here is it used to emphasize the Christ who emptied and humbled himself.

have overcome the evil one." If evil permeates the world, then 1 John 5 reassures us that "everyone who believes that Jesus is the Christ has been born of God. . . . Whatever is born of God conquers the world. And this is the victory that conquers the world, our faith. Who is it that conquers the world but the one who believes that Jesus is the Son of God?" (5:1–5).

In Christ, sin, death, and the power of evil have been defeated, and yet just as Christians continue to sin, evil still exists in the world. We do not fully understand. We do know that the effects of evil enter everyone's life, if not personally, in devastating ways, then collectively. John writes with assurance, "The one who was born of God protects them, and the evil one does not touch them. We know that we are God's children, and that the whole world lies under the power of the evil one. And we know that the Son of God has come and has given us understanding so that we may know him who is true; and we are in him who is true, in God's Son Jesus Christ. He is the true God and eternal life" (5:18–20). The battle with evil has been definitively won through Jesus Christ's death and resurrection.

Therefore, "Beloved, do not imitate what is evil but imitate what is good" (3 John 11); "Submit yourselves therefore to God. Resist the devil and he will flee from you" (Jas 4:7); and finally, "See that none of you repays evil for evil, but always seek to do good to one another and to all" (1 Thess 5:15).

- Recall or notice times when the news singles out certain people as evil. Think of examples of all of humanity's participation in evil in the world.

- How does Christ's victory over evil empower us with courage to challenge forces of evil and to transform people's lives and our systems of corruption, deception, war, and more?

Kenneth: Not Alone in Mission

Ben tells of walking with Kenneth: "Kenneth is a retired state trooper who grew up in New Jersey. He joined the air force and served in the Vietnam War. Ken is an active church member, spending his time on volunteer activities there and throughout the community in Wisconsin where he now lives. On a normal day one is likely to see Ken at the local diner. Then he works his way around town, talking to people, which makes him a very informed man. Ken has an openness to talking about faith and his commitment to social justice.

"I had Ken pegged completely wrong. I assumed he would fit the rural/small-town stereotype, not really paying attention to much outside of his own life. However, when I asked Ken about how his faith informed his ethics, he had a great deal to say about the world. He is deeply passionate that faith and ethics have everything to do with farming and feeding the world. He was also in tune with the changing racial demographic in his community and is committed to making immigrants feel welcomed in the community and especially in their church. He sees being an advocate for justice as part of his calling.

"We are not able to deal with the systemic evils of the world alone. Once any one person really opens up to the problems of the world, the problems become so numerous that any change seems hopeless. Ken realizes there is no reason to even try if we must go about it alone. But this is not the case. We are the people of God, one body with many and various parts, and we do not even have to figure out how to tackle the mountain of problems in this world all by ourselves. Jesus is the head and we are part of him; therefore, we are not alone in mission. Together we can take on the forces of evil that can seem overwhelming."

59. Merely Human/Servants of Christ

God created us human beings, and God called this creation good. Christ Jesus entered the human form: incarnation. However, in the Epistles one image for the human predicament is being *merely* human. "For when one says, 'I belong to Paul,' and another, 'I belong to Apollos,' are you not merely human?" (1 Cor 3:4). We are, according to Paul, behaving according to "human inclinations," meaning that we are making judgments and decisions on the basis of our limited—some might say self-centered—interests.

Although the word "flesh" is used frequently in the Epistles and could be an English synonym here, as well as "sinful self," I have decided not to follow those terms. I believe they may confuse or distance people whom we are trying to reach with the word of grace. People, however, are concerned about being merely human, not good enough, or wise enough, or holy enough for God. Once again the "mind of Christ" passage is helpful in that "Christ Jesus, who, though he was in the form of God . . . emptied himself . . . being born in human likeness. And being found in human form, he humbled himself . . . " (Phil 2:5–8). God created humankind in God's own image, but when it became tainted with sin, Christ humbly put on a human form. Through his cross we have become new.

This new image is to be a servant of Christ: "Of this gospel I have become a servant according to the gift of God's grace that was given me by the working of his power" (Eph 3:7). Paul and other writers refer to themselves as "servants of Christ" or "servants of God" (e.g., Rom 1:1; Titus 1:1; Jas 1:1; 2 Pet 1:1; Jude 1). Often, brothers and sisters in Christ are referred to as "fellow servants" or "beloved fellow servants" (e.g., Col 1:7; 4:7). And we are called "through love [to] become slaves [servants] to one another" (Gal 5:13).[6] We are, by grace, made and then called to be "servants of God" (1 Pet 2:16), loving the family of God and ministering in daily life.

- Have you heard someone refer to herself or to another as "merely human"? Was it out of self-deprecation? Helplessness? Was it used as an excuse? How else did you hear it?

- Christ's incarnation (becoming truly human for us) and his death and resurrection have transformed us for servant ministry in the world. What are the many ways we can see that?

Dick the Servant Banker

I talked with Dick at the Easter breakfast in his small-town church. We had met years ago, but still he remembered me and came up to greet me. We caught up on news of his daughter and then talked about issues of economic and income inequality. He mentioned the economic hardships and inequities his daughter, a pastor, was dealing with in her congregation and added, "We deal with that in our congregation here, too."

I asked him more. He told me he was in agricultural finance and went on to say that during the farm crisis of the 1980s it was tough. He remembers sitting at the kitchen table of a family. He had been working with them to help them keep their farm, but they weren't going to make it and he said, "It's time we talk about another calling for you and your family." Calling. The people who are fulfilling their callings in daily life helping others discern theirs, and during critical times. I was moved by his story. Then it was

---

6. In the RSV and the NRSV there are some differences in translation between verb and noun forms of "servant" and "slave." I am not citing all of the NRSV references to "slave."

time to go upstairs to the Easter Sunday service in the sanctuary. This was a resurrection, new hope story.

After the service, I looked around to find him so I could follow up on our conversation. I asked if I could share his story. He quickly said yes and then went on to say more. "I didn't go into banking to become a minister. But during those difficult days of the farm crisis, when I would have to go to the home of a farmer with the bad news, I made sure I didn't leave until some other person came home to be with him. I would never leave him alone," he said. I could see the pain and worry in his eyes still after all these years and understood how he must have felt merely human in the face of the many farmers committing suicide in those days. Now, these many years later, this servant of Christ, with tears in his eyes, still cared. "Sometimes I stayed a long time . . ." he said.

60. Cowardice, Foolishness/ Power of the Cross and Resurrection

Who wants to look like a coward? Who wants to be seen as foolish?[7] Both describe someone who lacks power or status, someone at whom others laugh. Everyone has had the unfortunate experience of looking foolish, if only for a moment, and who among us has not at some time felt like a coward? But for some this may be an ongoing human predicament. To think of oneself as being weak because one has become a Christian, in the way Christianity is often stereotyped, is not good news at all. This may be a particular barrier not only for men but for some women as well.

This image of the power of the cross and resurrection may be a very useful one to just such a person. "God did not give us a spirit of cowardice, but rather a spirit of power and of love and of self-discipline" (2 Tim 1:7). This verse is followed quickly by the words, "but join with me in suffering for the gospel, relying on the power of God" (v. 8). It must be said here that we include this image not to promote being change agents in the world through violence, or "conquering for Christ," or through the use of power and oppression. These are mission strategies that stain the history of the Christian church. Rather, this is to encourage the meek, the fearful, those of

---

7. "Ignorance" and "foolishness" are words from the Epistles used in the image of "Unenlightened/Wise" in chapter 2. Here we focus on "foolish" as it is used today, particularly in relation to having no power.

us who feel insecure in believing that God can empower us to make a real difference for good in the world.

Paul writes in 1 Cor 2:3–5, "I came to you in weakness and in fear and in much trembling. My speech and my proclamation were not with plausible words of wisdom, but with a demonstration of the Spirit and of power, so that your faith might rest not on human wisdom but on the power of God." So we together say, "I want to know Christ and the power of his resurrection . . ." (Phil 3:10).

- Have you ever felt like a fool? A coward? What does it mean to you to have the power of Christ in you? (What does it *not* mean?)

- When has a faith community lived too cautiously, too fearfully, rather than relying on the power of Christ to step out into the world and step up to working for justice?

61. Loser/Victorious

For all of the hymns portraying Jesus as our King victorious, this is a rather minor image in the Epistles. The image begs the question, over whom or what is Jesus victorious? And if there is a victor, who is the loser, or who has been conquered? "Thanks be to God, who gives us the victory through our Lord Jesus Christ" (1 Cor 15:57). God gives the victory to us *through* Jesus.

Life in the United States is all about winning and losing. After an important event, whether a soccer game, county fair, or community forum, people ask one question: Who won? Losing a game, a contest, a job, or a lover comes to define one's identity: "He/she is a loser." Being victorious is all about winning *against* someone else, or some other team or company. One aspect of the human predicament is that being victorious can so easily slip away. Victory can be a trap. Being a loser can be an indictment.

In fact, when being a Christian is associated with being weak, merely a servant, it can be equated with not being a real winner in the world's eyes. So one might want "a little Christianity" for one's children while at the same time wanting them to win at sports or other competitions so that they make it in the "real world." We therefore have two polar opposite false images of Christianity: being a weakling, a "loser," and the oppressive history of being conquerors for Christ.

Christ's victory is over the powers of death and all legal demands upon us, over rulers and authorities, over anything that would hold us captive.

God made us alive together with Christ. The image of victory is that the record that stood against us with its legal demands was nailed to the cross. "[God] disarmed the rulers and authorities and made a public example of them, triumphing over them in it." This is the central meaning of victory (Col 2:13–15).

In Philippians Paul writes about "pressing on," but he adds, "not that I have already . . . reached the goal." He is not writing about being victorious over others. "Christ Jesus has made me his own" (3:12). He says, "I press on toward the goal for the prize of the heavenly call of God in Christ Jesus." The point is to "fight the good fight of faith; take hold of the eternal life, to which you were called and for which you made the good confession in the presence of many witnesses" (1 Tim 6:12).

The image of victory or triumph is used in connection with mission. "But thanks be to God, who in Christ always leads us in triumphal procession . . ." (2 Cor 2:14). This does bring to mind images of the church conquering nations for Christ at the point of a sword. But actually the verse goes on, "and through us spreads in every place the fragrance that comes from knowing him. For we are the aroma of Christ to God among those who are being saved and among those who are perishing." Fragrance![8] And a few verses later we read, "For we are not peddlers of God's word like so many but in Christ we speak as persons of sincerity, as persons sent from God and standing in his presence" (v. 17). The image for mission may be victorious, triumphal procession, but at the expense of others losing either their lives or their culture. Rather, the victory is the victory of the open tomb, life for all, in Christ.

- How has a culture of winners and losers contaminated our attempt to have life together in community in the world?

- What does being part of Christ's victory over death mean for living and sharing life, the good news, with others in ways that respect who they are and the cultures from which they come?

Joan on Jury Duty

Brian writes of his walk with Joan in daily life: "The jury selection room was full when I arrived, so I chose a seat close to the back. I sat down and began

8. As noted in the introduction, there are more images in the Epistles than are contained in this book. One that was considered for inclusion was "fragrance."

reading the book I had brought with me. I felt as though the individual next to me was looking over my shoulder. I continued reading until I couldn't concentrate any longer because the person was reading my book. I felt a little embarrassed, but that's how I met Joan. She had been called for jury duty six times throughout her life, but had never been selected. She was, however, interested in the process. We talked.

"Throughout the morning we watched the selection process unfold. The case was one of domestic assault. The accused defendant sat with his back to us the whole time as the prosecuting and defending attorneys asked questions of the potential jurors. We were faced with making a decision about another human being's innocence. It was hard to remember that at that moment legally he still was. Joan is a Christian and I'm sure that was part of her decision-making process, but I don't know in what way that guided her answers to the questions being asked of her. We didn't have op-portunities to discuss grace or forgiveness. Would this trial be about who among the lawyers would be a winner and who would be a loser? Would we, if we were selected, become mediators of justice?

"I saw a humility about Joan that I associate with mercy in a very faithful way, faithful to her vocation as a citizen of this country and her vocation as a child of God called to judge another human being in a court of law. She didn't know if she would be chosen or not, or whether the case would be criminal or civil. She walked into that courtroom knowing only that her peers had called upon her and that she had a duty to fulfill, and she was willing to do so."

62. Disconnected/Mediated

When two parties are in dispute, or cannot be reconciled in their differ-ences and difficulties, they are in need of a mediator. "For there is one God; there is also one mediator between God and humankind, Christ Jesus, him-self human, who gave himself a ransom for all . . ." (1 Tim 2:5)

Christ is "the mediator of a new covenant, so that those who are called may receive the promised eternal inheritance . . ." (Heb 9:15). This image is repeated later in Hebrews: Jesus is "the mediator of a new covenant . . ." (12:24).

In a section in Galatians (3:15–29) regarding Abraham and the cov-enant God made with the Hebrew people, as well as questions about the place of the law, Christ is portrayed as a "mediator" (v. 19). This was "so that what was promised through faith in Jesus Christ might be given to those who believe . . . so that we might be justified by faith" (vv. 22–24). Thus the image of mediation connects believers in Christ with God, and also with the people of the promise who came before. Not only that, but the passage goes on. In Christ we are no longer disconnected from one another, "for in Christ Jesus you are all children of God through faith" (v. 26). "There is no longer Jew or Greek, there is no longer slave or free, there is no longer male and female; for all of you are one in Christ Jesus. And if you belong to Christ, then you are Abraham's offspring, heirs according to the promise" (vv. 28–29).

- From whom do you feel disconnected? When have you felt disconnected from God? Why?

- What have been your experiences with mediation and mediators? Imagine Christ as the ultimate mediator between you and God and among all of your human relationships.

Change Agents as Ministers of Reconciliation

In each of the images in this chapter, Jesus Christ, through the power of the Spirit, transforms Christians to be change agents in the world. These missions and ministries in daily life may take many different forms and even go in various directions. Central, however, is the ministry of reconciliation: between God and humankind, and among human beings. Vocation is rooted in the forgiveness on the cross and in the resurrection.

This forgiveness results in reconciliation. God, in Christ, has entrusted us with the ministry of reconciliation: "All this is from God, who reconciled us to God's own self through Christ, and has given us the ministry of reconciliation; that is, in Christ God was reconciling the world to Godself, not counting their trespasses against them, and entrusting the message of reconciliation to us. So we are ambassadors for Christ, since God is making God's appeal through us; we entreat you on behalf of Christ, be reconciled to God. For our sake, God made him to be sin who knew no sin, so that in him we might become the righteousness of God" (2 Cor 5:18–21).

Ron and Greater Grace

On Saturday, August 9, 2014, in Ferguson, Missouri, unarmed eighteen-year-old Michael Brown was shot and killed by a local policeman during daylight hours. Mike had been stopped for walking in the middle of the street. The issue was soon brought to the country's attention because this suburban community of twenty thousand just north of St. Louis is not the only place in the United States that faces issues of mistrust between citizens and law enforcement, systemic racism, and the militarization of police. Citizens protested, using the words, "hands up, don't shoot." (Mike had his hands up in compliance when shot.) When large numbers of protesters came, and it looked as though the situation might descend into lawlessness, local police responded with high-powered artillery, military vehicles, tear gas, and guns aimed at the citizens. Governor Jay Nixon called upon Missouri Highway Patrol Captain Ron Johnson to take over. He demilitarized the police reaction.

How do you become a minister of reconciliation in a dangerous situation? On August 14, Ron walked with the people in their peaceful protest, believing they should have freedom of assembly and expression. That night, there was calm for the first time since the shooting. The governor and Ron held a press conference on Friday morning during which they took questions from the people, not just the press.

Responding to a question, Ron recounted how he had returned home late Thursday night. His daughter, a recent college graduate, had asked, "Daddy, were you scared?" Ron went on: "I said, 'Just a little bit.' She said [drawing on Matt 14:22–33, the gospel text that many churchgoers had heard the Sunday before], 'Daddy, I want you to remember when Jesus asked Peter to walk with him on the water, Peter got scared. Jesus picked him up and said, 'Have the faith.'" Ron went on, "And I'm telling you today we need to be just like Peter because I know we're scared and I know we're falling, but he's going to pick us up and he's going to pick this community up."[9]

Due to some actions on the part of local police, the town saw more lawlessness in the following nights, even though the majority of the protesters in the community remained peaceful. Johnson continued to believe in community policing, even when the temptation to violence and military

9. My transcription of Ron Johnson's remarks to the public, August 15, 2014, outdoors, center of Ferguson, Missouri.

response was great. The following nights there was more violence. On the following Sunday, thirteen hundred people gathered at Greater Grace Church for a Unity Rally. Up to two thousand more gathered outside the church. Early on, Ron Johnson, introduced by the pastor to address the assembled, was welcomed with a standing ovation Here are his words, spoken extemporaneously:[10]

"I want to start off talking to Mike Brown's family. My heart goes out to them. I'm sorry. I wear this uniform and I stand up here and say that I'm sorry [*huge, appreciative applause*]. This is my neighborhood. You are my family. You are my friends. And I am you. I will stand to protect you, to protect your right to protest. I'm telling you I'm full right now. I came in here today and I saw people cheering and clapping. This is what the media needs to put on TV [*big applause*]. The last twenty-four hours have been tough for me. I did an interview last night and the reporter said, 'What's wrong? Your tone has changed.' He said, 'Are you tired? Or is something bothering you?' I said, 'My heart is heavy because last night I met some members of Michael Brown's family.' They brought tears to my eyes and shame to my heart. But I can tell you—and I talked to you about this before [*knowing applause*]—my daughter talked about a text about Peter and Jesus. She said, 'Daddy, I know you are going to be scared.' I'm not scared for me but scared for us. She said, 'When Peter failed, Jesus picked him back up.' I needed today to get back into the water. And I'm telling you I'm going to be here for as long as it takes. My words will be honest. If we talk behind closed doors I'm going to tell you. So if you don't want me to know, don't talk to me behind closed doors [*long applause*].

"When this is over, I'm going to go into my son's room, my black son [*cheers*], who wears his pants sagging, his hat cocked to the side, got tattoos on his arms, but that's my baby. And we all ought to be thanking the Browns for Michael. Michael's going to make it better for our sons, so they can be better black men, better for our daughters so they can be better black women, better for me so I can be a better black father, and we know he's going to make our mamas even better than they are today. Let's continue to show this country, this nation, who we are.

"When these days are over and Mike Brown's family is still weeping, no matter what positive comes in our lives, we still need to get on our knees. We need to pray. We need to thank Mike Brown for his life and we need to

10. My transcription of Ron Johnson's address at Unity Rally, Greater Grace Church, Ferguson, Missouri, August 17, 2014.

thank him for the change he's going to make that is going to make us better. I love ya. I stand tall with you and I'll see you out there [*standing ovation*]."

The days ahead would be hard, very hard. Ron Johnson would continue his ministry in daily life of leadership in difficult and dangerous times. One man's ministry. One man's witness. Greater grace.

CHAPTER 8

More Images than
We Can Imagine

In this final chapter the images are not centered on one central theme. One reason is that they simply do not come together easily that way. The second reason is that there really are more images than we can imagine in the Epistles. Discovery is open-ended. I trust that you, the reader, will discover more images yourself. You may, however, find some subtle pairings in this chapter. The stories, too, may connect in subtle ways. With shorter, minor images, the stories are a bit longer. Read and enjoy, and perhaps you will see new connections from stories of your own life.

Jesus alone is the faithful High Priest, but the emphasis in the Epistles is not on singular ordained priests but on the universal priesthood of all believers. Jesus the Priest is also Jesus the Pioneer. Because Jesus died not on an altar but "outside the city gate," we are to follow the Pioneer of our salvation into the world. Some people worry that their faith will not be sufficient or sustainable. Hardened hearts do not change the heart of God, nor does our unfaithfulness change the faithfulness of God. Paul makes it clear that we do not have a righteousness of our own based on how good we are or on how much we try to measure up. Jesus' act of righteousness leads to justification and life for all. People wander away from the gospel, following other goals or gods, perhaps without even realizing it at first. We are not likely to simply return on our own. But Christ does not forget us. "For you were going astray like sheep, but now you have returned to the shepherd and guardian of your souls" (1 Pet 2:25). We have never done so much damage that we cannot be returned to the one who was and is and will be the guardian of our souls. We are rooted in Christ and grounded in love.

63. Ineffectual Priesthood/Holy Priesthood

Not surprisingly, Hebrews uses this image extensively. However, we begin with two passages from 1 Peter: "Come to him . . . let yourselves be built into a spiritual house, to be a holy priesthood, to offer spiritual sacrifices acceptable to God through Jesus Christ" (2:4–5); "But you are a chosen race, a royal priesthood, a holy nation, God's own people . . ." (2:9). By grace, we (notice the plural) have become the priesthood of all believers, a central Reformation breakthrough. All Christians are called to be a holy priesthood and to proclaim the mighty acts of God. Within the baptized, the *laos,* some are set apart for public ministries of word and sacrament and word and service, but the emphasis in 1 Peter 2 is not on singular ordained priests, but on becoming God's people, the universal priesthood of all believers through the forgiveness of sins on Christ's cross alone.

Erica the Principal

Nancy writes about her walk with Erica in daily life: "Among the priesthood of all believers carrying out their vocations in daily life is Erica, a middle school principal. She works with sixth, seventh, and eighth graders in a rapidly growing school district. She arrives at school at 7:30. She says she would like to arrive by seven, but first she needs to drop off three of her children at day care. He husband takes the older two children to school a little later. Erica ends her day at her school in time to pick up all five by 5 p.m. There are evenings when she returns to school after putting her children to bed. She finds her best time to finish paperwork is when there are no interruptions. Those nights she tries to finish by midnight—so she leaves when the night janitors leave. The sign outside her office door may explain why she doesn't have much 'behind the desk time' during the day. It reads, 'Students are not an interruption of our work, but the purpose of our work.'

"I arrived at my appointment with Erica about fifteen minutes early and was greeted warmly by the office staff. Erica was out visiting classrooms. About five minutes later she returned and started talking about her concern that students don't feel they are being challenged enough on a daily basis. She and I visited five sixth-grade classes that morning, not staying long. It was interesting to see the different methods the teachers were using. Erica met privately with one teacher later in the day and explained to me that she is trying to help this teacher think about how students view an activity.

"It was now time for eighth-grade lunch. There is 'group lunch,' a 'homework lunch' for those who have not completed assignments, and a 'quiet lunch' for those who have a hard time tolerating noise. We visited each type, one each for sixth, seventh, and eighth grade. In all three situations I observed Erica interacting with students in a personal way. She greeted them by name and made sure she was at eye level, not standing over them.

"Erica began her career as a sixth- and seventh-grade teacher and enjoyed that but felt she wanted to make a difference in the lives of teachers and students that she could not do as a classroom teacher. She seemed surprised that as I watched her I saw a connection between her work and ministry. She is faithful in her daily life, ministering to students and staff as she guides, comforts, and cares for them."

Jesus the Faithful High Priest

The Letter to the Hebrews is concerned to make clear that Jesus is the one high priest who was faithful (3:1–2); he is not one who is unable to sympathize with us, but "one who has been tested, as we are, yet without sin" (4:15). Formerly, the priest was chosen "from among mortals" and "had to offer sacrifice for his own sins as well as for those of the people." But Christ was "designated by God" and, "having been made perfect, he became the source of eternal salvation for all who obey him" (5:1–10).

People today—as in ages past—have doubts about the trustworthiness of their leaders. Are the leaders effective? Can they be trusted? Are they people of truth and ethics? Do they represent God's will for my life? Hebrews makes the case for Christ being different: "We have this hope, a sure and steadfast anchor of the soul, a hope that enters the inner shrine behind the curtain, where Jesus, a forerunner on our behalf, has entered, having become a high priest forever according to the order of Melchizedek" (6:19–20).[1] Christ "holds his priesthood permanently, because he continues forever" (whereas former priests were "prevented by death from continuing in office"). "Consequently he is able for all time to save those who approach

1. Read Hebrews 7 for more on King Melchizedek.

God through him, since he always lives to make intercession for them. For it was fitting that we should have such a high priest, holy, blameless, undefiled, separated from sinners, and exalted above the heavens" (7:23–26).

This makes all the difference in the world—for our worship, for our faith, and for our lives in the world. "Therefore, my friends, since we have confidence to enter the sanctuary by the blood of Jesus, by the new and living way that he opened for us through the curtain (that is, through his flesh), and since we have a great priest over the house of God, let us approach with a true heart in full assurance of faith. . . . Let us hold fast to the confession of our hope without wavering, for he who has promised is faithful" (10:19–23).

- Think about the leaders, the "priests" you have known in the church (perhaps you are one). Each one clearly is not Jesus, and yet, how do they seek to serve in Jesus' name? How can we help them, and ourselves, be faithful to our great High Priest?

- The priesthood of all believers is a powerful Reformation breakthrough, though one not totally realized or utilized. How might we more fully claim and sustain vocations of all believers empowered by the forgiveness of sins, which comes straight from Christ alone?

- What kind of leader was Erica as a principal? What kinds of leaders are we?

64. Left Back/Pioneer of Salvation

This image follows the one before, not obviously in content, but in the context of Hebrews. "Therefore, since we are surrounded by so great a cloud of witnesses, let us also lay aside every weight and the sin that clings so closely, and let us run with perseverance the race that is set before us, looking to Jesus the pioneer and perfecter of our faith . . ." (12:1–2). Jesus the Priest is also Jesus the Pioneer. Because Jesus died not on an altar but "outside the city gate" (13:13), we are not to be left back inside the city, inside the sanctuary. We are to follow the Pioneer of our salvation: "Let us then go to him outside the camp and bear the abuse he endured" (Heb 13:13).

We are to "pursue peace" (12:14). "Let mutual love continue. Do not neglect to show hospitality to strangers, for by doing that some have entertained angels without knowing it. Remember those who are in prison, as though you were in prison with them; those who are being tortured, as though you yourselves were being tortured" (13:1–3). "It was fitting that God, for whom and through whom all things exist, in bringing many children to glory, should make the pioneer of their salvation perfect through sufferings" (2:10).

We enter the sanctuary but do not stay there. "Go in peace. Serve the Lord." "Go in peace. Share the good news." "Go in peace. Remember the poor." Marge Leegard, a faithful servant of Christ, would say, "We say these things to one another as we are dismissed from worship, but when we return the next Sunday we are never asked, 'Did you?'"

- A pioneer leads us forward. Where and how far will Christ, the Pioneer of our faith, lead us this week?

- When Jesus leads us "outside the camp," how might we support one another in working for justice in the world?

Trey and Bach in the World

After Carter's ride-along with his friend, Trey, Carter told this story: "Trey and I have become work buddies at a local restaurant where we both are servers. One night I approached Trey and said I had a strange question to ask. 'What do your Tuesday mornings look like at your other job?' He answered, 'Tuesday mornings are crazy busy.' I said 'Would it be possible for me to go to work with you?' He replied, 'I usually leave town by 6:30. Is that too early?' 'Nope' I answered. 'OK, I'll pick you up,' Trey said. Later that night he said, 'Are we going to talk about theology?' 'Yeah, if you want to,' I replied. 'Then we will definitely talk about Bach!' he exclaimed.

"Trey arrived early Tuesday morning and we headed off. He is a professor of music at a small state university about half an hour away and is also the conductor of a city choral group here as well as in that university town. Trey lives in the world for the purpose of music. I asked if he had a church affiliation. His answer revolved around music. He said he had worked in many churches but claims no church of his own. He said he believes in the triune God but that God's nature is ultimately unknowable.

"That morning I watched Trey teach his classes for people preparing for careers teaching music in elementary school settings. He seemed a gentle and excited teacher, imparting the importance of music education in children's lives. Trey told me later he tries to cultivate a sense of awe in students. 'I don't see awe very much in our world. I try to communicate through music the rare sense of wonder, of the unexplainable. Many of my students seem to have a jaded worldview.' Trey tells his students that music does not exist on the page. 'It is something alive, living in the world. It is too wonderfully complex to happen on its own. Whether we write it down or not, music would still be there. The same is true of God. Whether we can describe God or not, God still exists."

65. Hardened Hearts/Firm Confidence

If grace is a gift, does God thrust salvation upon us? Can we refuse it? The Epistles use the image of hardened hearts not open to God's unconditional love, or of hearts once open that have closed. Christ was faithful: "Therefore, as the Holy Spirit says, 'Today, if you hear his voice, do not harden your hearts as in the rebellion, as on the day of testing in the wilderness . . .'" (Heb 3:7–8).[2] A few verses later, in a caring way, the reality of falling away is set before us: "Take care, brothers and sisters, that none of you may have an evil, unbelieving heart that turns away from the living God. But exhort one another every day, as long as it is called 'today,' so that none of you may be hardened by the deceitfulness of sin. For we have become partners of Christ, if only we hold our first confidence firm to the end" (3:12–14). And then is repeated, "Today if you hear his voice, do not harden your hearts as in the rebellion." Ephesians 4:18 also uses the image of "hardness of heart."

We are also encouraged: "Do not, therefore, abandon that confidence of yours; it brings a great reward. For you need endurance . . ." (Heb 10:35–36). Faith is a gift of grace and firm confidence, sustaining confidence even more so. Which brings us to the familiar passage, "Now faith is the assurance of things hoped for, the conviction of things not seen" (Heb 11:1).

Some people worry that their faith will not be sufficient or sustainable. In a long passage in Romans about the Jews, Gentiles, and the law, one verse needs to be read in that context but also is true in any circumstance: "What if some were unfaithful? Will their faithlessness nullify the faithfulness of God?" (3:3). Our hardened hearts do not change the heart of God, nor does our unfaithfulness change the faithfulness of God. By Christ's faithfulness we become faithful. We do not have to muster up enough faith or even ready our hearts for God's love. God's love initiates our faith and breeds our confidence. God is steadfast, so that "by steadfastness and by the encouragement of the scriptures we might have hope" (Rom 15:4–5).

2. Quoted from Ps 95:7–11.

- Do you at times worry that your faith is growing cold and your heart is becoming hard? Take confidence in your faithful God and in the steadfast love of Christ Jesus.

- To what brother or sister in faith might you turn when you need your confidence strengthened?

66. Unrighteous/Righteous through Faith

The word "righteous" today is often used to say someone appears "self-righteous," a characteristic not to be admired. However, in the Bible, to be righteous, or "right with God," was very important. And in that sense, so too today. Paul makes it clear that we do not have a righteousness of our own based on how good we are or how much we try to measure up to the law. So, too, we cannot ever measure up to any set of moral standards, to the Ten Commandments, or to an ethics of perfection. A person's own un-righteousness may drive him to adopt a façade of self-righteousness. Paul writes that his is not "a righteousness of my own that comes from the law, but one that comes through faith in Christ, the righteousness from God based on faith. I want to know Christ and the power of his resurrection . . ." (Phil 3:9–10).

Unrighteousness is not to be taken lightly. It is more than wrong actions; it can be a powerful delusion, leading people "to believe what is false, so that all who have not believed the truth but took pleasure in unrighteousness will be condemned" (2 Thess 2:11–12). In Romans Paul makes the case that through the law came the knowledge of sin. "But now, apart from law, the righteousness of God has been disclosed, and is attested by the law and the prophets, the righteousness of God through faith in Jesus Christ for all who believe. For there is no distinction, since all have sinned and fall short of the glory of God; they are now justified by God's grace as a gift, through the redemption that is in Christ Jesus . . ." God did this to show God's own righteousness and that God "justifies the one who has faith in Jesus" (3:20–26).

Paul goes on, saying, "so one man's act of righteousness leads to justification and life for all" (5:18). "For all" is made specific: "Gentiles, who did not strive for righteousness, have attained it, that is, righteousness through faith" (9:30). This distinction is made yet again in Rom 10:5–10, in which Paul writes about the righteousness that comes from faith, the "word of faith that we proclaim" (v. 8), "because if you confess with your lips that Jesus is Lord and believe in your heart that God raised him from the dead, you will be saved" (v. 9). Faith is "reckoned as righteousness" (4:5). This is the gospel, "For in it the righteousness of God is revealed through faith for faith; as it is written, 'The one who is righteous will live by faith'" (1:17).

No one else but Christ does God describe as righteous. "For to which of the angels did God ever say, 'You are my Son; today I have begotten you'? . . . But of the Son God says . . . the righteous scepter is the scepter of your kingdom. You have loved righteousness and hated wickedness" (Heb 1:5–9). The scepter and crown of righteousness that belong to Christ will be reserved for those who believe in him, as 2 Timothy concludes: "I have kept the faith. From now on there is reserved for me the crown of righteousness, which the Lord, the righteous judge, will give me on that day, and not only to me but also to all who have longed for his appearing" (4:7–8).

Two familiar passages make very clear that we are reconciled to God on behalf of Christ: "For our sake God made him to be sin who knew no sin, so that in him we might become the righteousness of God" (2 Cor 5:20–21). We not only have righteousness but *become* the righteousness of God! And this brings life: "The one who is righteous will live by faith" (Gal 3:11).

Sidney on Fridays

Rob watched and learned from Sidney. Here is his story: "Sidney works part-time for an Internet provider as an internal mediator for their personnel services department. She is an empathetic listener with high social intelligence. She decides based on complaint report documents who will meet with her about a given dispute. Sometimes she meets with one party, often both, and sometimes they all three meet together.

"She has to be there on Fridays because terminations are carried out Friday mornings and one of her duties is to pack up the personal effects of such employees so that they can be shipped to them at home via courier. The corporate policy is that when people are notified of termination they are escorted off campus by security immediately. This work is part of Sidney's vocation.

"As an internal mediator Sidney decides what sorts of conversations will help guide participants to functional settlement. She does not determine or recommend for termination; therefore employees know she is a safe person in whom they can confide. At first Sidney was reluctant to accept my use of 'call' language in regard to her position, but the more we spoke about it the more she seemed to agree. On our ride home she said, 'I just never really thought of my job as anything special, but when you talk about it as spiritual and vocational, I can agree with that.'

"Sidney's approach to the human predicament seems to be that we should try to get along, but when we cannot it's 'best for everybody' if the person 'who has to move on' moves on. A little more than 50 percent of her cases do end in termination. The good news in Christ she brings is that disagreements occur and there is grace on a personal level even in the firings. They may not be right for the company but they are no less righteous before God in Christ.

"I watched her pack up people's belongings all day and she was always intentional and careful with things; she reminded me of a funeral parlor person. Close coworkers often interrupted her packing. Some shared their own remorse or upset feelings. Sin within this setting is cast as 'it could happen to anyone' ideation. There was no, 'Well, all they had to do was X and they would still have a job' kind of language. Sidney speaks corporate and kindness languages. She acknowledged to me the sadness of her Friday packing but said that even people who were fired would sometimes drop her a letter or e-mail about how much her taking the time to pack their things up right made them feel better."

The New Life of Right Relationships

The First Letter of John describes this new life of righteousness by grace through faith as resulting in right relationships and actions. In Christ there is no sin or unrighteousness, and no one who abides in Christ continues to abide in sin. "Everyone who does what is right is righteous, just as he is righteous" (3:6–7). We can never be "right enough" to be righteous before God, but abiding in the righteousness of Christ leads to doing right. We can grow in righteousness. "All scripture is inspired by God and is useful for teaching, for reproof, for correction, and for training in righteousness, so that everyone who belongs to God may be proficient, equipped for every good work" (2 Tim 3:16). Likewise, "you may share abundantly in every good work. As it is written, 'He scatters abroad, he gives to the poor; his righteousness endures forever.' He who supplies seed to the sower and bread for food will supply and multiply your seed for sowing and increase the harvest of your righteousness" (2 Cor 9:8–10). "And a harvest of righteousness is sown in peace for those who make peace" (Jas 3:18).

- How have you seen in yourself or in others the journey from "unrighteous" and "self-righteous" to abiding in the righteousness of Christ? In what ways have you sown seeds for a harvest of righteousness?

- If Christ, who knew no sin, became sin (unrighteous) for us, how does that change the way we live?

67. Wandering/Brought Back

Many congregations and church bodies in recent years have experienced decline as people leave, or "wander away." Where do they go? For what reasons? Individuals may wander away from the truth of the gospel, following other goals or gods, perhaps without even realizing it at first. People may experience lives of wandering from one pursuit to another, from one church to another, or away from church altogether. Some churches have a "welcome home" invitation at Christmas, trying to reach and recover those who have not been seen in the Christian community for some months, or perhaps for years.

"My brothers and sisters, if anyone among you wanders from the truth and is brought back by another, you should know that whoever brings back a sinner from wandering will save the sinner's soul from death and will cover a multitude of sins" (Jas 5:19). Such a small image in the Epistles and yet such a potent one for the church today. So easy to leave, so easy to be not noticed, so easy to be forgotten. This passage makes clear that one is not likely to simply return on one's own. The good news is that we belong to each other through baptism and are part of the body of Christ forever. Christ does not forget us. As we commune "in remembrance" of Christ, Jesus feeds us with his body and blood so that we might also "remember one another" and reach out to bring back the one who has wandered away.

- Who is missing from your community of faith? Whom have you not seen for a few weeks? Who has been gone for so long that their names have almost been forgotten?

- To whom might you reach out? How? How might you as brothers and sisters do this together, formally and informally?

Sue's Passion for Youth

Paul writes about the challenge of vocation: "Sue is a nurse in a small hospital. She works part-time because of her diagnosis of multiple sclerosis roughly twenty years ago. The time of her diagnosis was challenging. She was bedridden for more than three months. Three older children were fairly self-sustainable; their youngest son, Jimmy, was only four. It was beautiful to hear Sue speak of the love that was shown by not only her family but also by people of her church community at that time of great life change. For one, her husband, Bill, had to learn how to cook and care for her family around the house while working full-time as a technology support manager. (Bill now loves to cook!)

"Parishioners quickly signed up to assist with basic home needs such as getting Jimmy ready for school. Members sent meals during those first most difficult months. Sue said, 'We felt so loved and we realized the importance of a faith community in times of difficulty. It wasn't just the meals; it was a faith support, too.'

"Through all of these years living with MS, Sue's passion in her vocation was particularly evident in the energy she expressed for teaching confirmation classes to eighth-grade students. She has been teaching every year for almost twenty-five years. Sue said, 'I really enjoy teaching them about the love God and how we are called to be channels of God's love for the people we meet. I tell them that this love is especially important for the people they meet in school.'

"Sue spoke of the challenge of high school students wandering away from the church following their confirmation. For Sue, the grief she feels as students leave is a result of her deep connection to the students and her personal passion for the Christian faith. She loves those youth and wants the best for them and feels being part of the church is important for all people and especially for young adults in our society. Sue and Bill spoke of intentional mentoring of young adults inside and outside the classroom setting. Bill said, 'I try to say hello to the young guys, just to see how they're doing.' Sue and Bill are people who may not fully know the importance of their ongoing connection with young people. As Sue said, 'I don't do a lot, but I do what I can.'"

68. Going Astray/Returned

The work of Christ is portrayed in so many different ways, often linked together in one section of Scripture. In 1 Pet 2:23–25 we see the abused Christ who suffered on the cross. By his wounds we have been healed. We read, "For you were going astray like sheep, but now you have returned to the shepherd and guardian of your souls" (v. 25). This image is similar to the previous one, but also different. To go astray carries the implications of leaving Christ, scattering in all directions. We may run, or walk. We may become lost. We may find ourselves in danger in a thicket, or in dangerous company. Our lives may spiral downward until we are unrecognizable to others and even to ourselves. How did we become lost in the first place? How did it begin? Is there no way to find our own way back to safety, to sanity, to community?

The gospel is that Christ is the guardian of our souls and of our lives, now and into eternity. Now, adults may not want a "guardian," as that sounds as if we are incapable of living on our own. But the truth of the matter is that we are not capable of fully directing our own lives. Christ looks for us. Thanks be to God. We never have gone too far astray. Our lives are never in too much of a mess. We have never done so much damage that we cannot return, or be returned, to the one who was and is and will be the guardian of our souls. That is indeed forgiving, good news.

- Have you ever gone astray? How far?

- Do you worry about, long for, someone you know who has gone astray? Do you wonder how in the world you can reach him or her? What difference does believing that Christ is still his or her guardian make in your relationship?

Harry and His Forty-Thousand-Acre Ranch

Sam accompanies Harry across the miles and tells this story: "Harry is the patriarch of a four-generation ranch that covers more than forty thousand acres. Some of the movie *Dances with Wolves* was filmed in the immediate area. Harry has now passed full-time management of the ranch to his oldest son, Dwayne.

"We took off in the morning into one of the north pastures, looking for both deer and cattle. The ranch primarily raises calves in the pastures to be sold to finishing feedlots across the Midwest. I asked Harry, 'Have you ever wanted to do anything else other than ranching?' He replied, 'I don't know what else I'd do. I've lived here my entire life. I was riding a horse when I was three. Nowadays kids learn about dirt and cattle and plants at college, but they don't *do* it. The guys that write those books live in a lab; they don't come out here and live on the land; they don't know how to love the cattle the way I do.'

"In my years of knowing Harry I had seen his first concern was for the cattle and the land. Gates and fences are carefully shut. Stock dams are created to capture runoff water the few times that it rains. We drove through the north pastures, viewed a few mule deer at a distance and saw what Harry expected to see—plenty of contented cattle grazing in pastures that had benefited greatly from some late summer rains.

"We moved on south and Harry told me, 'Don't worry about shutting the gate; we moved all the cattle out of here two weeks ago.' This was even rougher terrain than the pastures to the north. Then I noticed through my spotting scope what looked like a yellow cattle ear tag. I turned to Harry and said, 'You said you moved all the cattle out? I see one down in the bottom, about a half mile east of here.' We started out and as we came up over the final hill, I saw Harry's body slump in reaction to what he saw. The cow had worked herself into a wet spot at the bottom of a wash and sunk. All we could see was her head and neck; her body was buried in the loose shale and gumbo.

"Harry said nothing but drove as near to her as he could, climbed out of his pickup, grabbed a chain, wrapped it around his hitch, walked over to the cow, talking to her the whole time, trying to console her. He wrapped the chain around her neck, put the truck into low gear and slowly pulled her out. He unwrapped the chain and tried to encourage her to get up. She was severely emaciated and covered in mud and bodily waste. Harry got down on his knees and tried to help her, bending her limbs. I could see tears in his eyes. He walked back to me at the pickup and pointed at the rifle in the truck. With a catch in his voice and tears in his eyes, he asked me if I could end her suffering because he said he could not do it himself. I did as he asked. As we left the pasture, Harry was silent. We sat together, and I could tell he was mourning.

"Later that day I asked him what he felt was his calling as a rancher. He replied, 'To care for the land and the animals God has given me.' Harry and his family live and breathe with the land and their cattle. This is a tough land on which to make a living. Water is hard to find. Harry and his sons do their best to steward the land and the livestock, of course, but also the pheasants, grouse, geese, ducks, deer, and antelope with which he believes he has been entrusted."

69. Cursed/Blessed

Cursing is a common practice, acceptable in some circles but not in others. Some would say it doesn't mean much. Whether we use "curse words" or harbor cursed thoughts, it is a widespread practice in this and every age, and our words and thoughts have consequences. In some ages and cultures, people believed that they had the power to actually put a curse on another person. Even if that is less true in our North American culture today, there are many people who believe their lives are cursed. They believe there are powers that control their lives and they simply cannot break out to live a happy, "blessed" life.

"Christ redeemed us from the curse of the law by becoming a curse for us—for it is written, 'Cursed is everyone who hangs on a tree'—in order that in Christ Jesus the blessing of Abraham might come to the Gentiles, so that we might receive the promise of the Spirit through faith" (Gal 3:13–14). Although this is a very minor image in the Epistles, it is a powerful one. Christ became a curse for us. Think of the all-encompassing meaning that might have for anyone who has ever felt, or who now feels, that they live a cursed life. Christ does not shun or judge. He has compassion, but more than that, he becomes the curse on the cross.

For those who experience "curse" more as being forever condemned, Paul's words in Rom 8:1 are good news: "There is therefore now no condemnation for those who are in Christ Jesus." Grace means being set free from curse, condemnation, and death. Such release is real and can be believed.

The image of being blessed permeates the Epistles. Here are but a few examples: "Blessed be the God and Father of our Lord Jesus Christ, who has blessed us in Christ . . ." (Eph 1:3); "For the grace of God has appeared, bringing salvation to all, . . . while we wait for the blessed hope . . ." (Titus 2:11–13). The new life in Christ does not mean that every day will be a happy day free of pain and suffering. "But even if you do suffer for doing what is right, you are blessed" (1 Pet 3:14). Grounding our lives is the blessedness of forgiveness: "Blessed are those whose iniquities are forgiven, and whose sins are covered" (Rom 4:7).[3]

3. Paul quotes Ps 32:1

Having been blessed with a blessing that can overcome any feeling of being cursed, our vocation is now to be a blessing, to live careful and caring lives, knowing the power of both cursing and blessing; for, as James writes, "no one can tame the tongue . . . with it we bless the Lord and Father, and with it we curse those who are made in the likeness of God. From the same mouth come blessing and cursing. My brothers and sisters, this ought not to be so" (Jas 3:8–10).

- In your daily life, what encounters with cursing, either verbal or mental, do you experience, participate in, or observe? What effects does it have on people's lives?

- How are you a blessing to others, and how might you be in ways that you are not yet? Who is a blessing to you?

Matthew the Reporter

Ryan sees the world through Matthew's eyes and tells the following story: "I'm sitting in a spinning desk chair watching Matthew type up notes from a reporter's interview earlier that day. He laughingly says that reporters' handwriting is almost as bad as doctors'. Matthew, twenty-seven, a copy and design editor for a publishing company that owns papers all over the country, is waiting for one last article to come in so it can be formatted for a daily newspaper that will be printed in Missouri.

"I met Matt almost eight years ago. He attends worship services but is not a member of a church. This past summer we often had conversations about our interests, work, and faith over coffee and pancakes in the early mornings as he was getting off work, since he works the third shift at the paper. I asked Matt how his faith played a role in his job and he seemed to be uncomfortable with the question. He diplomatically answered that he did not think it did. I told him of course it did. We proceeded to talk about storytelling. We both like to tell stories, so the conversation lightened. Matt told me one connection he sees between his job and his faith would be storytelling. We talked about the Bible's being a narrative, how it is the grand story of salvation wrapped around smaller stories. Stories of war, of love, of greed, of curses and blessings, of messed-up people with whom almost anyone can identify in some way. Matt said that the newspaper is sort of the same way. They publish these pages daily or weekly because people want to know the news and there are lots of small stories, too. Stories of the global world and the local world where people live. The papers bring them good news and bad news.

"I said something to the effect that newspapers often deliver bad news, unlike the Bible, which shows the good news to all of humanity. Matt disagreed, reminding me that there is plenty of bad news about the human condition in the Bible, too. He then said this: 'Newspapers might bring bad news or good news, but either way they let people know they are not alone. They keep people connected . . . and I think the Bible does the same thing. It lets people know they are not alone in the world. That someone cares. That God cares about them when the rest of the world does not seem to care.'"

70. Rootless/Rooted

We live in a mobile society and have for some decades. We speak about wanting to "put our roots down" but also desire the freedom to be innovative and to live with endless opportunities. For some, to be rootless is a kind of bondage even as they seek it. Meanwhile, refugees from war and impossible economic circumstances have had their roots severed. Whole groups of people and thousands, sometimes even tens of thousands from a single nation become homeless and therefore rootless. On an individual basis, due to abuse or alcoholism or homelessness, people are rootless. Or a person may say she is psychologically rootless. The human predicament is varied and real.

To say "God forgives you" to people in these difficult circumstances may not make sense. Worse yet, it may be an offense. God becomes more distant, less understanding, someone left behind in a far-off, once safe country. The image of grace is that even while we are uprooted, or rootless for any reason, no one can uproot us from the love of God in Christ Jesus. Paul prays for the Ephesians that they may be strengthened in their inner being with power through God's Spirit "and that Christ may dwell in your hearts through faith, as you are being rooted and grounded in love" (Eph 3:16–17). When the hurricane blows through, or the tornado uproots our homes, we are still rooted and grounded in the love of God.

We also are encouraged to continue to live our lives rooted in Christ; God, who established our faith, continues to build that faith. "As you therefore have received Christ Jesus the Lord, continue to live your lives in him, rooted and built up in him and established in the faith, just as you were taught, abounding in thanksgiving" (Col 2:6).

- This very day, millions of people around the world find themselves homeless, uprooted. How are we part of the problem? How might we participate in providing a rooted belonging?

- Have you been or are you now rootless, in any sense of the term? What does it mean to you that you have been rooted and grounded in love by Christ Jesus?

Pam, Cheerios, and the Unknown

Anna walks where Pam walks and writes about her daily life: "The air blows briskly through the neighborhood. The last stream of sunlight disappeared hours ago. The night envelops everything at this hour. Pam finally has time for our visit, if that visit includes cleaning, picking up and putting away, doing laundry, catching up on e-mail, schoolwork, job applications, and grocery shopping.

"Pam spends most of her day in her primary vocation as mother of three little ones under the age of three. When she opens the door for me, I see books, stuffed animals, and Legos intermingled indiscriminately. Cheerios have been cast about without a care. Pam and Tom stand, two survivors of tonight's toddler tornado. All but one of the little guys has drifted to sleep. Tom waves us out the door. Tonight the necessary task that our visit includes will be shopping. We hop in the car, the headlights gleaming the way to our mercantile mecca. We have a special mission tonight. We will not only buy diapers but will also search for professional attire for Pam.

"After months of searching Pam has a job. As we move from the stylish skirts toward the diapers, Pam shares worries about what the next year will bring. Her family needs the income, but they also need her. This will be the first time since the birth of her children that she will not spend every day with them. We remember to dash over to the grocery section before leaving.

"Pam recalls the time she took her little ones to worship. Sitting in the back, she had planned to keep them occupied with their favorite finger food. The plan worked too well: instead of eating them, the little ones began flinging them. Little snack puffs bounced through the pews, across the aisles, and even toward a parishioner or two. Pam rounded up the rowdy little crowd and spent the rest of the service in the narthex.

"Reaching the end of the lists, we pass through the checkout. We hop in the car. At the end of it all, we offer each other prayer, intending to keep each's other health and sanity in mind and heart. The chaos of the unknown threatens to destroy the structure she has built. The storm of uncertainty rages as she tries to navigate a troubling job market and a demanding family role. As she runs from errand to errand, chasing children and employment, she longs for breath and calm, for renewal and steadfastness.

"Just where is God in the 9 p.m. errand run? Where is God in the unemployment and the unanswered wait? Where is God in a divided yet discerning heart? Pam searches for a firm foundation. Even in the middle of these stormy and chaotic scenes, God provides a rootedness in Christ beyond anything else."

Guides for Engagement

B ooks are books, most often read alone. These guides for engagement are intended to turn this book into an event, most often a communal event. Many of the ideas provided below you may already be doing in one way or another. My hope is that these guides will enrich and strengthen your life together for deeper growth in faith and for further ministry in daily life.

1. Learning Together

Whatever the time and place for teaching and learning, setting and maintaining a trustworthy environment is all-important. Questions for reflection and conversation are provided with each image. Questions come alive way beyond words on the page when people engage each other in a trustworthy environment. In such an environment we observe confidentiality, talk honestly, listen respectfully, speak for ourselves, and do not presume to know what others are thinking or what they have experienced. Here we give room for the Spirit to be present and to transform our hearts through the power of the living God. The open-ended questions are appropriate for cradle Christians and for those whose walk with Jesus Christ has just begun or who are contemplating the Christian faith for the first time. This book is not dependent upon a certain level of biblical knowledge. All can learn together because all have real lives.

People who are not acquainted with the Bible or the church but who have observed Christianity in the culture may perceive of God as a judgmental God, or of Christ as "the good example Jesus." Biblical illiteracy is an issue, but just as significant in this competitive society is the foreign nature of the concept of unconditional love by a gracious God. Providing a trustworthy environment where people can encounter a broad range of images of grace that meet their own human situation and hear others' stories has the potential for them to open their own life stories and to encounter a God to whom they can relate.

For people who have been away from the church for a while (whether years or decades), either one on one or in a small group the chapters in this book can provide opportunity to let go of some painful experiences of the past—perhaps when they felt alienated from the church, or when the church seemed a waterless place, or unforgiving, or when they felt the burden of shame. Specific images may provide ways to encounter the grace of God anew: such as belonging, life-giving, unconditional acceptance, and a place to finally let go of shame. All of this can become not just something known by the intellect but felt and experienced in a trustworthy, caring learning community.

A campus ministry setting or a formal college religion class would most likely include people of various religions or those who say they are spiritual but not religious (the "nones"). This introduction to the New Testament Epistles is different from an historical introduction to the Christian Bible. A leader or teacher could invite personal storytelling of the human predicament, both personal and systemic, through deep listening alongside biblical exploration. Respectful discussion rather than argumentation would be essential.

Within a Christian faith community, such as a Bible study group, a pastor's class, an adult study forum, or peer support group, one would not present this book through lecture. Methods could include going through one chapter per session and having various people prepare and present images of their choice, sharing biblical work and further examples. Open-ended discussion would be a key method. The questions are not framed for "yes or no" or "right or wrong" answers. A teaching leader should not ask "guess what I'm thinking" questions. Rather, the goal is to draw people in more deeply and draw forth conversation. The teaching leader will be learning along with everyone else.

The goal is not to finish the question but to allow the conversation to flow, making sure everyone has a voice and no one dominates either in opinion or stories. This can be achieved by people going around the group initially and "speaking themselves present" with a simple, direct question such as, "To which image in this chapter did you relate, and why?" Once a person in a group has spoken once, she or he is likely to speak again. Participants need to own their ideas and stories. (There is no place for someone to say, "You will find that in life . . .")

When a group is larger than five or six, the use of dyads or triads is particularly useful for part of the session. At various points, simply have people turn to each other in twos or threes and talk about one question, particularly one that might be hard for some to talk about in the whole group—for example, "Share a time when you have been rejected. How does this image speak to that experience?" (Image 41) When returning to the large group, people may share what they have spoken about in the dyad or triad, but there should be no requirement to do so.

This book has been used in seminary and pastoral and diaconal continuing education settings. While it helps ministers think about the laity with whom they work (see "walking with" below), I have found that ministerial leaders start engaging the book to think about their own lives. We are all part of the *laos*, with many arenas to our daily lives.

2. Using an Image

People with whom I have used this material become engaged in one of two ways: 1) they look at one image and think, "How does this image relate to me?" or 2) they look through the list and find an image that fits the situation of someone about whom they care. And often, on the way, they stop at an image that speaks to their own personal story right now. In either case, they are ready to explore more deeply what Scripture has to say.

As I said in the introduction, we engage people with the images by starting either with the stories of human lives and people hungering for the grace of God or with the scriptural images. If we begin with the human situation, we cannot simply look for an "answer" in Scripture, in a proof-texting way. Nor should we take one of the images and project it onto someone as though we had all the answers for their life. The goal is to look at and listen to people as we meet them on the road in daily life.

Not all of the images will relate to everyone; however, everyone can benefit from becoming aware of the broad range of images of salvation in the Epistles. So, to just pick and choose one or two would short-change a study group. In a pastoral care situation, selecting one image might be precisely what is called for. A study group might work their way from chapter 1 to chapter 8, or they might want to select where they begin. Memorizing the images is not the goal. Becoming fluent with possibilities in order to use them in ministries in daily life would be a good outcome. A group might want to engage in role playing, imagining how conversations could go. One person might speak about a real or fictitious life situation while another listens. As they converse, they would encourage one another by speaking about the grace of God in an image that speaks to that particular need. This may feel awkward at first, but over time people will become more skilled in talking about God's grace in Christ in a broader range of images.

As a group continues to meet together, they could begin sessions by sharing experiences from their time apart. "What images of the human predicament did you notice this week? What images from the Epistles might have spoken to that situation? Were you able to speak about Christ in that situation in a way that directly related to the need there?" From that initial exchange, deeper conversation and further growth in skill could emerge, as well as further biblical study. I have seen and heard ordinary people use the biblical images in authentic conversation, and once they do, they continue to do so. This also impacts how they listen to sermons, hear the news, and interpret global events. All of this equips them for ministry, for mission, and for becoming agents of justice in a world in need.

3. Walking With

Clergy often make pastoral care visits, but they may be less comfortable entering the worlds of people in the various arenas of their daily lives. Diaconal ministers may be more likely to minister in the community, bringing the needs of the world to the church. Still, it is rare that the laity experience "professional" ministers simply walking with them in their worlds outside the church, listening and watching. How does one start? What does one do there? How does one not get in the way?

Jesus walked the dusty roads with people, conversing with them as he went. We can, too. And Christians can walk with each other—watching, listening, caring, asking, accompanying. In chapter 3, Image 20, we read the story of Renee, Ben, and Jonathan in Haiti during the 2010 earthquake. Before they went they were often asked, "What are you going to do there?" Their answer was that they were in a ministry of accompaniment, a term used in our church in global mission. They were there accompanying, making relationships, learning from the people of Haiti. This is incarnational, "being with." In so doing, we witness grace in the midst of the most devastating and the ordinary. In our walking with, we go as who we are, but not to give pastoral advice; we go as a friend, and we are there to learn.

Over the years I have walked with more people than I can count in their arenas of daily life and have been with "Connections"[1] groups making visits to places of people's ministry in daily life. Whether it was sitting with a woman on her porch in inner-city Detroit, listening to a school social worker's story in Orlando, Florida, admiring a Denver city librarian's sense of call to the homeless who came in, or hearing about the life of a newspaper publisher in his office high over the city of Oakland, California, I remember vividly what I heard and learned. Almost always the people would say they discovered things about themselves as they spoke in their words, in their place.

Are some places inaccessible? Not really. Sometimes one does have to make arrangements, and one must always be very respectful. Sometimes permission is required in order to be there. But one can walk with quietly, simply observing, and have a conversation in a side room or nearby café afterwards. Once in a while we would go to the place of work after hours, but still we could "see" what went on there. The arenas of vocation, as one could see in this book, include places of paid or volunteer work, leisure, home, and more. Just talking *about* people's daily life in the church classroom or fellowship hall is not nearly as effective as actually going there and walking together. Sometimes spending time in more than one arena, as was the case with Larry in chapter 1 (Image 5, Old Covenant/New Covenant), can add dimensions not present in just one. Most important is authenticity—and, before and afterwards, appreciation.

This is how one woman described walking with: "It was an honor to have an extended amount of time to walk with a man whom I thought I knew well. I discovered the foundation we already had allowed the experience to be one of profound connection and actual ministry beyond what I ever anticipated. Along the route to visit three of the distributors of his products, his story began to unfold. . . . In telling how he develops relationships, we landed smack dab in the middle of a theological discussion. I was entering a whole new dimension of discussion. I listened intently as he

1. *Connections: Faith and Life,* 3rd ed., copyright Evangelical Lutheran Church in America, 2011, is now a web-based resource, with permission granted for personal and congregational use. It is an experiential education resource consisting of four units, with six sessions per unit, that helps people connect faith with ministry in daily life and involves visits to people's places of vocation. It is currently housed on the website of Wartburg Theological Seminary.

opened up about all sorts of thoughts, concerns, and questions he had about his faith. The key factor in this ministry opportunity was that I entered his world and walked with him there. This allowed him to fully engage in an honest, truth-centered conversation."

"I experienced a holy time with this man, quite honestly, a time that was unexpected and one for which I had felt a bit unprepared at the outset. However, relying upon the presence of the Holy Spirit, I listened and listened some more, allowing the conversation to flow until it slowed. We shared how we placed our trust in the truth of Christ Jesus. The visit ended with a long time of silence between the two of us before the normal routine of saying goodbye."

In her description, she quoted from a book I coauthored with Craig Nessan titled *Transforming Leadership*—in this case, on the importance of establishing trust and honoring people: "Only by investing heart, mind, and soul in relationships with people one serves, and by doing so over time, can one attain the social capital needed to engage in mutual transforming ministry."[2] In writing about listening in a person's language, she added a second quote: "Through this experience, I recognized the importance of listening, especially in light of my inclination to jump in and offer a counter to questions that surface. 'People will tell you what you need to know, if you are ready to listen to them.'"[3]

4. Listening in the Language of the Other

The woman quoted above listened while riding along with a businessman. But what if we do not know the language of sales, of the pharmacy or the farm, of education or engineering? We will not know all those languages, or the distinct "dialects" of each—for example, medicine is a broad field with many different disciplines. But we can listen to the language of the other. And unlike an English-speaking person trying to understand a French-speaking person, we will be able to understand fairly well. It is the terms that are foreign, and their usage. Perhaps also the goals and values. We are tempted to *think* we understand, but a word may be used differently from one context to another. Thus the need to observe and notice and, yes,

---

2. Norma Cook Everist and Craig L. Nessan, *Transforming Leadership* (Minneapolis: Fortress, 2008) 4.

3. Ibid., 25.

appreciatively inquire. As we uncover the differences, the misunderstandings, it is amazing how we open up new insights for others and ourselves.

In pastoral care, or peer support groups, the focus will be to listen for something in the other person's story. The goal is to help people discover images that name their own experiences. Helping them claim their image is quite different than naming it *for* them or using the Bible *at* them. The goal is to claim and name and acquire new meaning for themselves. One needs to be careful not to project. For example, I may hear a story about a situation that mirrors a situation I have been in. I may presume that the other person is experiencing "meaninglessness" there, but that may not be the case; they may feel a sense of purpose there.

Carefully listening to each other sounds so easy, but that is not the way most engagements go. Most often we pass each other in parallel conversations. You speak about something in your life, and that sparks an experience of mine, which might or might not directly connect. Too often, at least in U.S. society, conversation is a competition. In a fast-paced, electronically connected society, meeting face to face and really listening long and deep has become a skill to relearn. When we do, we discover new insights about the depth of systemic sin, the complexities of global issues and human relationships, and together, new insights about the grace of God. God's unconditional love can come alive anew.

5. Discerning Vocations

One arena of *vocatio* is the service we do within the faith community for building up the body of Christ. There are many books describing how ministerial leaders can identify, equip, support, and recognize those faithful servants who minister within the congregation. I myself teach courses in educational ministry, church administration, and leadership. However, in this book we have seen that the broader perspective is to see that the ministry of the baptized extends to all the world. Each time we gather for worship, we are sent forth with words such as, "Go in peace. Share the good news." Or, "Go in peace. Remember the poor." Then we return again from our roles and relationships to the gathered people of God, not just for worship but for education, for service projects within and on behalf of the congregation, for care for one another, and more. We are not just isolated individual congregations but part of larger church bodies, able to do all sorts of education, equipping, and service together. This work is essential, but not just for sustaining the church itself; always for the church and all its members being the body of Christ in its myriad arenas in daily life. The three "body of Christ" passages (see Image 37, Uselessness/Gifts) ground us, especially Eph 4:1–16. The emphasis of ministry within the church is "to equip the saints for the work of ministry, for building up the body of Christ" (v. 12) and to promote "the body's growth in building itself up in love" (v. 16) so that together the community can make all the difference in the world.

Martin Luther wrote about our "stations" and "vocations." In today's language we would call stations the roles and relationships where we live in the arenas of our daily lives. Everyone has a particular station—in fact, we have multiple stations in our complex lives. When speaking about vocation, in this book I have used the Latin term *vocatio* to distinguish it from the English usage, which often is limited to a "profession" or "a religious vocation." Some people say, "I don't have a vocation; I just have a job." That is to miss the message. Each of us has many arenas of daily life. Each of us has many stations—roles and relationships. In each one there is potential for ministry. Our vocations (callings) are related to our particular stations and rooted in our new life in Christ.

Some people separate callings by saying that first there is our calling of the gospel to faith and second there are our stations in relation to creation, namely, our callings in the world. That is to separate the external, daily life from the "spiritual." Although Luther did write about two realms (kingdoms), Einar Billing notes that "when it began to dawn on Luther that just as certainly as the call to God's kingdom seeks to lift us infinitely above everything that our everyday duties by themselves could give us, just that certainly the call does not take us away from these duties but more deeply into them." God's calling and earthly work are "inseparably united."[4] I do not see a separation in Scripture. In fact, I see the Christ who put on flesh and walked the roads everyone else walked. No matter where we are, in our many stations (situations, roles, and relationships), we are in need of repentance and forgiveness in Christ. That is why it is so very important that we take the emphasis on ministry in daily life one step further than simply talking about people serving in creation in the world. We need to help people discern what are the needs (human predicaments) and then,

---

4. Einar Billing, *Our Calling* (Rock Island, IL: Augustana, 1958) 5–6. Noted more fully in chapter 5

using many images in the languages people speak in daily life, ask what is God's grace and what are our callings (*vocatio*) in Christ there.

The following is an effective way to engage a group in such discernment to vocation. I have used this many, many times with groups small and large. Participants' ages, educational backgrounds, or cultural heritage are not barriers. In fact, variety enhances the experience.

Write the word "Station" at the top, on the left-hand side of a board or on newsprint, and underneath write the words "Roles and Relationships." Affirm the wide variety of roles and relationships in our lives, the challenges of each, and how many stations continue to change, some even while they remain the same. We may remain in the relationship of parent to three children, but our role changes from the time they were toddlers to when they are teens, and again when they are adults. You may point out examples from this book.

List some examples of stations in your life, and then have participants think about—or more helpfully, write on a piece of paper—their own list of roles and relationships (it may be long). Provide enough time for this, perhaps five minutes. Then invite participants to turn to each other in dyads and share from their lists, perhaps focusing on one or two roles in particular. We need the help of brothers and sisters in Christ to help us discern our ever-changing roles and relationships. Once again, provide a significant amount of time for partners to engage in conversation with one another. Then call the group back together and invite (do not cajole) participants to share a few stations and some of what they talked about with their partners. The goal is not to report everything but to affirm the variety of stations. All are potential places for our callings to ministry, to *vocatio*.

Now, on the top of the right-hand side of the board or newsprint, write the word "Vocation." In between "Station" and "Vocation," write "Grace," with "through Jesus Christ" underneath. Not everything we do in life is ministry, but in each of our stations there is potential for ministry, the *call* to ministry. And this calling is specific to the human need (the human predicament) at that time. For example, one might be sister-in-law for decades; the call to ministry now is her current health crisis. Another example is that one is a "citizen" (of one's town or city, one's state and country, the world itself). In the role of citizen, what is one's specific call to the ministry of justice right now?

Once again give a few examples from your own list of stations, perhaps only two or three, making clear they are to be thinking of their own lives, not yours. Here is the challenge, and it is a good one: if our call to ministry is rooted in the good news of grace through faith in Jesus Christ, what particular image of grace might be especially helpful in our call to ministry in this situation, in this time and place? Perhaps: "The situation in my complex family feels like one of bondage, but in Christ I am freed from the bondage of my own fear to ask my sister-in-law what she needs." Perhaps: "The amount of global turmoil and uncertainty leaves me feeling as if the world is shaking all around me. In Christ I have a firm foundation, not just for my personal life, but so that I can engage in global issues through my church body and through speaking out publicly on global policies."

Have the group think of some together. Then give time for individuals to ponder their own list of stations and identify one or two where they might think about their call to ministry. When each set of partners is ready, they may resume their conversation, helping each other discern their calls to ministry in the particular roles and relationships in which they live daily. After ample time for significant conversation, draw the participants back for group discussion and concluding words of encouragement. Close with prayer.

This is challenging work. It is real. By God's grace, in community we continue to discover the depth of the human predicament and the power of the gospel, thereby becoming equipped for vocation, which makes all the difference in the world.

Index of Epistle Passages

Index of Epistle Passages

Index of Stories

Introduction

Chapter 1

Chapter 2

Chapter 3

Index of Stories

Chapter 4

Chapter 5

Chapter 6

Chapter 7

Chapter 8

Index of Stories

CPSIA information can be obtained
at www.ICGtesting.com
Printed in the USA
LVHW100923050422
715333LV00005B/325

9 781625 647399